Types of word

A **noun** can be a thing, a place, a person or an idea you can think about.

An **adjective** describes a noun.

A **verb** is an action word.

An **adverb** tells you more about a verb or how, when or where something happens.

A **preposition** is a word that connects other words in a sentence to nouns.

noun

The silly clown balanced skilfully on his unicycle.

adjective   verb   adverb   preposition

What else can I find in this book?

More words to use

Scenes to write about

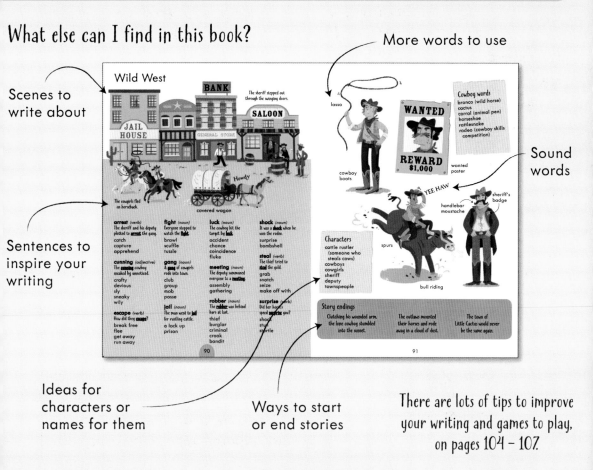

Sound words

Sentences to inspire your writing

Ideas for characters or names for them

Ways to start or end stories

There are lots of tips to improve your writing and games to play, on pages 104 – 107.

3

Contents

Size words

tall *(adjective)*

big
gangling
lanky
lofty
soaring
towering

long *(adjective)*
elongated
extended
lengthy
stretched

small
(adjective)
little
tiny
mini
dainty
miniature
minute
petite
puny
teeny
compact
wee

thin
(adjective)
narrow
slim
lean
skinny
slight
slender

big *(adjective)*
The orange-horned monster
is so **big**.

huge
large
gigantic
enormous
hulking
immense
bulky
mammoth
massive
overgrown
vast

short *(adjective)*
My legs are **short**.

squat
stubby
stumpy
squashed

fat *(adjective)*
chubby
chunky
flabby
hefty
large
plump
podgy
portly
stocky
stout

How big?

quite *(adverb)*
The green monster is
quite big.

a bit
a little
fairly
rather
somewhat

very *(adverb)*
The blue monster is
very big.

ever so
exceedingly
extremely
really
truly

How many?

few *(adjective)*
Few monsters
have horns.

a handful of
hardly any
not many
one or two

many *(adjective)*
Many monsters have tails.

a lot of
countless
lots of
numerous

Colours

Colours can be adjectives or nouns.

red	crimson	cherry	tomato	scarlet	ruby
maroon	pink	magenta	cerise	fuchsia	rose
salmon	coral	orange	amber	apricot	peach
ginger	yellow	lemon	butter	mustard	saffron
gold	ochre	buff	green	lime	acid green
grass green	bottle green	olive	khaki	emerald	jade
blue	turquoise	royal blue	azure	powder blue	sky blue
cobalt	navy	sapphire	purple	indigo	grape

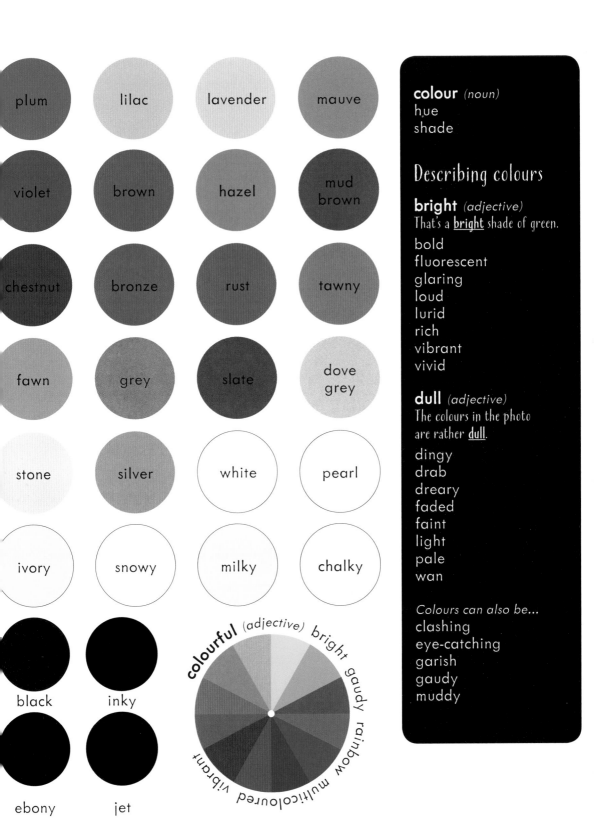

plum

lilac

lavender

mauve

violet

brown

hazel

mud brown

chestnut

bronze

rust

tawny

fawn

grey

slate

dove grey

stone

silver

white

pearl

ivory

snowy

milky

chalky

black

inky

ebony

jet

colourful *(adjective)* bright gaudy rainbow multicoloured vibrant

colour *(noun)*
hue
shade

Describing colours

bright *(adjective)*
That's a **bright** shade of green.
bold
fluorescent
glaring
loud
lurid
rich
vibrant
vivid

dull *(adjective)*
The colours in the photo are rather **dull**.
dingy
drab
dreary
faded
faint
light
pale
wan

Colours can also be...
clashing
eye-catching
garish
gaudy
muddy

Shapes

Flat (2D) shapes

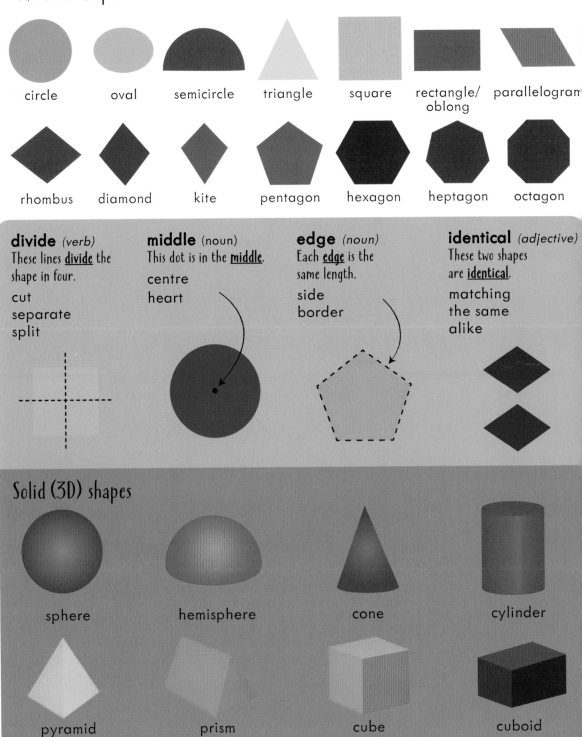

circle   oval   semicircle   triangle   square   rectangle/ oblong   parallelogram

rhombus   diamond   kite   pentagon   hexagon   heptagon   octagon

divide *(verb)*
These lines **divide** the shape in four.

cut
separate
split

middle *(noun)*
This dot is in the **middle**.

centre
heart

edge *(noun)*
Each **edge** is the same length.

side
border

identical *(adjective)*
These two shapes are **identical**.

matching
the same
alike

Solid (3D) shapes

sphere   hemisphere   cone   cylinder

pyramid   prism   cube   cuboid

Patterns

complicated
(adjective)
complex
fiddly
intricate
ornate

plain
(adjective)
simple
basic

curly
(adjective)
squiggly
swirly

spotty
(adjective)
dotted
flecked
mottled
specked
speckled

chequered
(adjective)
checked
harlequin
patchwork

slurp

stripy
(adjective)
lined
striped

even *(adjective)*
All of our patterns
are <u>even</u>.

balanced
uniform
regular

zigzag
(adjective)
jagged
wavy

Materials and tools

Things can be made from metal, wood, plastic, rubber, glass, paper, card, clay, fabric, leather, stone...

plastic *(noun)*
Types of plastic:
acetate
acrylic
perspex
polystyrene

wood *(noun)*
timber
planks

Types of wood:
ash
cherry
mahogany
maple
oak
pine
walnut

metal *(noun)*
Types of metal:
aluminium
brass
bronze
copper
gold
iron
lead
nickel
silver
steel
tin

fix *(verb)*
She had to <u>fix</u> the broken gate.
mend
repair
put right

toolbox

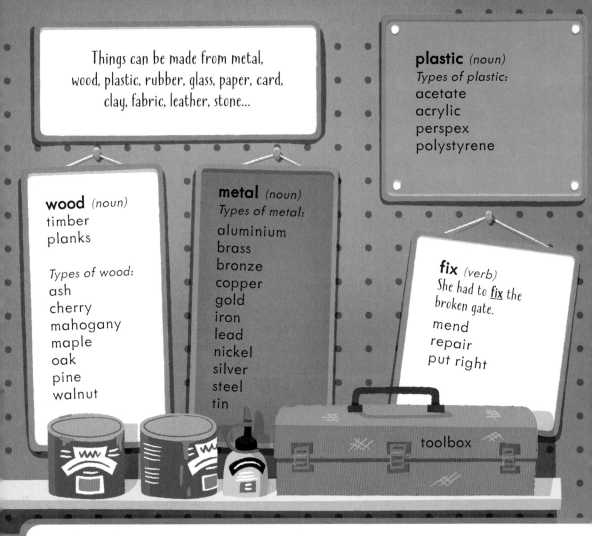

Describing how materials feel and look

bumpy *(adjective)*
knobbly
lumpy
ridged
uneven

clear *(adjective)*
see-through
transparent

cloudy *(adjective)*
murky
opaque

delicate *(adjective)*
breakable
brittle
flimsy
fragile

dry *(adjective)*
crisp
crispy
dried out
parched

fluffy *(adjective)*
furry
fleecy
downy
shaggy
woolly

hard *(adjective)*
firm
rigid
stiff

heavy *(adjective)*
bulky
hefty
weighty
dense

light *(adjective)*
easy-to-carry
lightweight

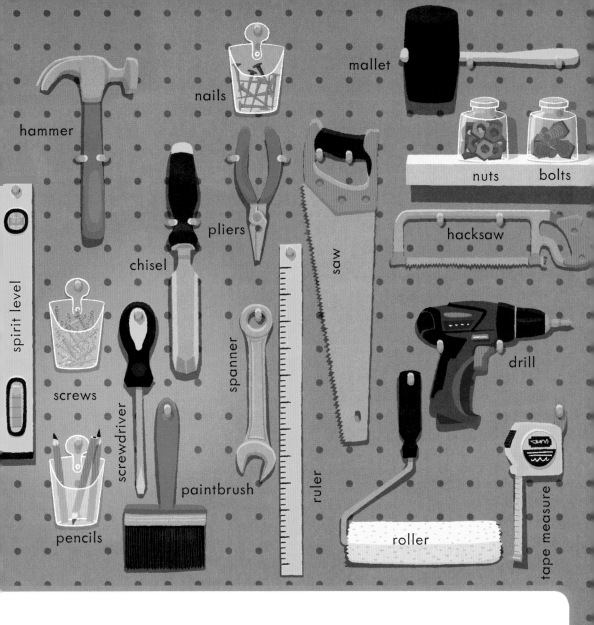

hammer
nails
mallet
nuts
bolts
pliers
chisel
hacksaw
saw
spirit level
screws
spanner
drill
screwdriver
paintbrush
ruler
pencils
roller
tape measure

rough *(adjective)*
coarse
craggy
gnarled
leathery
uneven

sharp *(adjective)*
spiky
jagged
pointed
scratchy
bristly
spiny

smooth *(adjective)*
even
glossy
polished
satiny
sleek

soft *(adjective)*
bouncy
squashy
springy
doughy

solid *(adjective)*
compacted
jam-packed
thick

strong *(adjective)*
durable
hard-wearing
solid
sturdy
tough

wet *(adjective)*
damp
dewy
moist
soggy
sodden

sandpaper

string

sanding
block

Giving opinions

opinion *(noun)*
What's your <u>opinion</u>?
feeling
point of view
view

believe *(verb)*
I used to <u>believe</u> this route was best.

think
be of the opinion
be sure
be convinced

better *(adjective)*
This way is <u>better</u>.

easier
more effective
preferable

fair *(adjective)*
I think a reward would be a <u>fair</u> idea.

appropriate
apt
deserved
fitting
just
proper
suitable

general *(adjective)*
The <u>general</u> opinion is that man's a liar.

common
typical
universal

hate *(verb)*
She used to <u>hate</u> olives.

dislike
despise
detest
abhor
loathe
have an
   aversion to

important
(adjective)
There's an <u>important</u> difference between the two.

critical
significant

like *(verb)*
I used to <u>like</u> chocolate.

enjoy
love
relish
be keen on
be partial to

We used to <u>like</u> her.

be fond of
be friends with
get on well with

Do you think they'd <u>like</u> it?

be interested in
take pleasure in

The children really <u>like</u> their granny.

adore
love

likely *(adjective)*
The <u>likely</u> result is their team will win.

probable

maybe *(adverb)*
<u>Maybe</u> it will be a draw.

perhaps
possibly

mind *(verb)*
Will you <u>mind</u> if I'm late?

be bothered
be upset
care
object

ordinary *(adjective)*
It's a fairly <u>ordinary</u> painting.

average
mediocre
unremarkable

possible *(adjective)*
Do you think it's <u>possible</u> we will lose?

conceivable
feasible

right *(adjective)*
She gave a <u>right</u> answer to the question.

correct
true
valid

seem *(verb)*
How does it <u>seem</u> to you?

appear
look

special
(adjective)
There's something <u>special</u> about this film.

exceptional
first-class
outstanding
unique
unusual

suggest *(verb)*
I <u>suggest</u> we go back before it's dark.

advise
propose
recommend
urge

unfair *(adjective)*
It's <u>unfair</u> that they can't come too.

unjust
unreasonable

wrong *(adjective)*
The boastful boy gave a <u>wrong</u> answer.

false
incorrect
untrue

Nice words

nice *(adjective)*

There's a **nice** view from my palace.

beautiful
breathtaking
glorious
picturesque
spectacular
splendid

He's a **nice** host.

courteous
gracious
polite

It was **nice** of you to lend me your guitar.

helpful
kind
likable
lovely
pleasant
sweet

The decorator did a **nice** job.

careful
neat
professional

We had a **nice** time at the show.

agreeable
brilliant
enjoyable
fun
good
great
lovely
marvellous
terrific
wonderful

That lunch was **nice**.

delicious
lovely
tasty

The weather is **nice** today.

beautiful
bright
fair
fine
glorious
lovely
mild

What a **nice** smell!

aromatic
fragrant

She's such a **nice** person.

amiable
caring
charming
considerate
delightful
friendly
generous
good-natured
helpful
kind
likable
lovely
pleasant
sweet
unselfish
warm-hearted

I look **nice** in my new suit.

attractive
beautiful
handsome
lovely
pretty
stunning

Good, bad or okay?

yippee

WOW

good
(adjective)

They gave a **good** reason for being late.

adequate
genuine
proper
reasonable
valid

The gardener did a **good** job.

admirable
careful
first-rate
satisfactory
sound
thorough

You're a **good** person.

decent
honest
just
upright
virtuous

We thought the book was **good**.

brilliant
excellent
fantastic
great
marvellous
super
superb
terrific
wonderful

The weather is **good** today.

bright
fair
fine
glorious
mild
sunny

They told some **good** stories about their trip.

entertaining
exciting
lively
vivid

My little brother is such a **good** boy.

angelic
helpful
lovely
polite
well-behaved

We had such a **good** time.

enjoyable
fun
interesting
pleasant

She's a **good** tennis player.

accomplished
capable
fine
first-class
gifted
talented

That was a **good** thing to do.

charitable
considerate
kind
thoughtful

You're in a **good** mood.

cheerful
cheery
happy
jolly
positive

YAY

bravo

14

HISS

yuck

bad
(adjective)

I've never read such a **bad** book.
- abysmal
- appalling
- atrocious
- dire
- lousy

This **bad** weather is depressing.
- awful
- dismal
- dreary
- foul
- nasty

There was a **bad** accident.
- catastrophic
- disastrous
- dreadful
- horrific
- serious
- terrible

A **bad** man ruled the country.
- corrupt
- cruel
- dishonest
- evil
- sinful
- wicked

My little sister is such a **bad** girl.
- badly-behaved
- cheeky
- disobedient
- mischievous
- naughty
- rude

The thief felt **bad** about his crimes.
- ashamed
- guilty
- terrible
- uneasy
- upset

The plumber did a **bad** job.
- abysmal
- dreadful
- inadequate
- inferior
- poor
- unsatisfactory

That's a **bad** habit.
- dangerous
- harmful
- risky

Why are you in a **bad** mood?
- irritable
- lousy
- sulky

A **bad** smell came from the bin.
- disgusting
- foul
- horrible
- repulsive
- revolting
- unpleasant
- vile

The old apples are **bad**.
- mouldy
- rancid
- rotten
- spoiled

meh

okay
(adjective)

I suppose the soup is okay.
- acceptable
- all right
- average
- O.K.
- reasonable
- so so
- tolerable

hmm

gah

bah

15

What are you like?

 err

 HOORAY

 grrrr

character *(noun)*
My oldest friend has a unique <u>character</u>.
nature
personality

boring *(adjective)*
dreary
dull
tedious

brave *(adjective)*
courageous
fearless
intrepid
plucky
daring

childish *(adjective)*
babyish
immature
puerile
young

clever *(adjective)*
bright
brainy
intelligent
sharp
smart
wise

clumsy *(adjective)*
awkward
bungling
uncoordinated

crazy *(adjective)*
insane
mad

curious *(adjective)*
interested
inquisitive

funny *(adjective)*
amusing
comical
droll
hilarious
witty

fussy *(adjective)*
choosy
fastidious
finicky
pernickety

generous *(adjective)*
charitable
kind
magnanimous

grumpy *(adjective)*
bad-tempered
crabby
cantankerous
surly
tetchy

honest *(adjective)*
honourable
moral
scrupulous
trustworthy
truthful
virtuous

kind *(adjective)*
caring
considerate
sweet
warm-hearted

lively *(adjective)*
bubbly
energetic
exuberant
sprightly

lovely *(adjective)*
amiable
charming
delightful
enchanting
engaging

naughty *(adjective)*
cheeky
disobedient
mischievous
unruly

nosy *(adjective)*
meddlesome
prying

polite *(adjective)*
considerate
courteous
respectful
well-mannered

proud *(adjective)*
arrogant
conceited
haughty
snobbish
snooty
vain

sensible *(adjective)*
level-headed
practical
thoughtful

serious *(adjective)*
dour
earnest
stern

shy *(adjective)*
bashful
coy
reserved
timid
wary

silly *(adjective)*
daft
featherbrained
foolish

stupid *(adjective)*
brainless
dim
idiotic
slow

How do you feel?

feeling *(noun)*
A strange <u>feeling</u> came over me.
emotion
sensation

brrrr

ARGHH

WAAAA

angry *(adjective)*
cross
enraged
fuming
furious
irate
livid

bored *(adjective)*
fed up
restless

cold *(adjective)*
chilly
cool
frozen

confused
(adjective)
baffled
bamboozled
bewildered
fazed
flummoxed
muddled
perplexed
puzzled

cross *(adjective)*
annoyed
grumpy
irked
irritated
vexed

dizzy *(adjective)*
faint
giddy
weak
wobbly

excited *(adjective)*
eager
ecstatic
enthusiastic
frenzied
keen
thrilled

full *(adjective)*
satisfied
stuffed
well-fed

happy *(adjective)*
cheerful
chirpy
delighted
glad
jolly
joyful
perky
pleased

hot *(adjective)*
feverish
flushed

hungry *(adjective)*
famished
peckish
ravenous

ill *(adjective)*
bilious
poorly
sick
unwell

sad *(adjective)*
depressed
down
forlorn
gloomy
glum
heartbroken
low
miserable

scared *(adjective)*
afraid
alarmed
disturbed
frightened
terrified

sorry *(adjective)*
ashamed
guilty

surprised
(adjective)
amazed
astonished
astounded
shocked
startled
stunned
thunderstruck

tired *(adjective)*
drowsy
exhausted
sleepy
weary
worn out

upset *(adjective)*
angry
hurt
shaken
worried

well *(adjective)*
fine
fit
healthy
in good shape

worried *(adjective)*
anxious
frantic
fretful
nervous
on edge
tense

People

baby *(noun)*
newborn
little one

child *(noun)*
boy
girl
infant
kid
toddler

teenager *(noun)*
teen
youth
youngster
adolescent

adult *(noun)*
grown-up

How people look

attractive
(adjective)
You're very <u>attractive</u>.
beautiful
good-looking
handsome
pretty

old *(adjective)*
His wrinkles made
him look <u>old</u>.
aged
elderly

ugly *(adjective)*
You're not <u>ugly</u>.
ordinary-looking
plain
unattractive

young *(adjective)*
She looks <u>young</u>
for her age.
fresh-faced
youthful

Writing about faces

face *(noun)*
I'd describe his
<u>face</u> as striking.
appearance
features
visage

Faces can be...
angular
babyish
chubby
flushed
freckled
oval
rosy
spotty
strong-jawed
stubbly
tanned
wrinkled

Features:
beard
cheek
chin
dimple
eye
eyebrow
forehead
freckle
moustache
nose
pimple
scar
spot
wrinkle

Pulling faces

scowl *(verb)*
Don't <u>scowl</u>!
frown
glower
glare

smile *(verb)*
Your aunt will <u>smile</u>
when she sees you.
beam
grin

Parts of the body

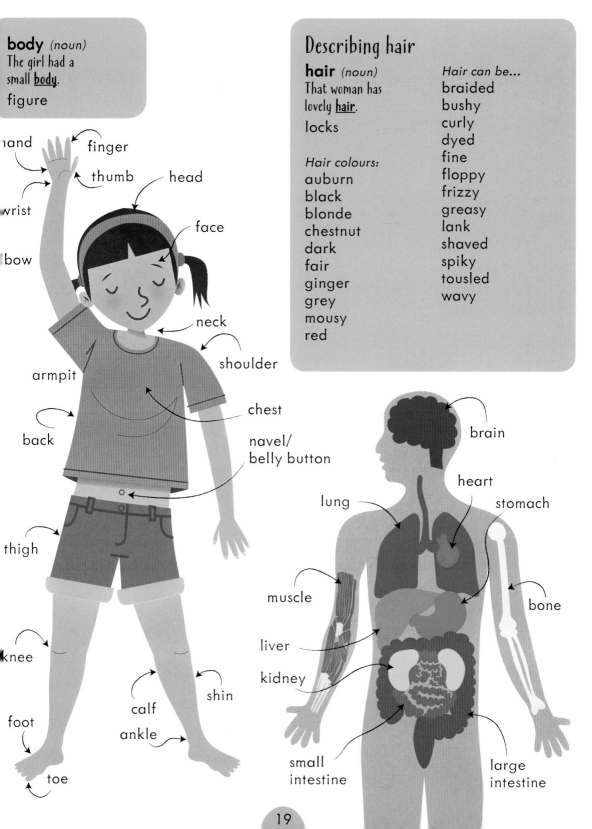

body *(noun)*
The girl had a small <u>body</u>.
figure

Describing hair

hair *(noun)*
That woman has lovely <u>hair</u>.
locks

Hair colours:
auburn
black
blonde
chestnut
dark
fair
ginger
grey
mousy
red

Hair can be...
braided
bushy
curly
dyed
fine
floppy
frizzy
greasy
lank
shaved
spiky
tousled
wavy

hand
finger
thumb
head
wrist
face
bow
neck
shoulder
armpit
chest
navel/
belly button
back
thigh
knee
foot
toe
calf
ankle
shin

brain
heart
stomach
lung
bone
muscle
liver
kidney
small intestine
large intestine

Flowers, plants and trees

flower *(noun)*
There was just one <u>flower</u> on the bush.

bloom

Types of flowers:

anemone
bluebell
carnation
chrysanthemum
cornflower
cowslip
crocus
daffodil
dahlia
daisy
forget-me-not
foxglove
freesia
geranium

hollyhock
hyacinth
iris
lavender
lily
lupin
marigold
orchid
poppy
rose
sunflower
sweet pea
tulip
violet

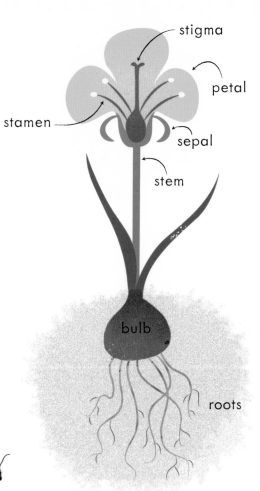

stigma

petal

stamen

sepal

stem

bulb

roots

A bumblebee made a gentle humming
sound as it flitted from flower to flower.

dandelion

The gentle breeze dispersed the seeds far and wide.

plant *(noun)*
Types of plants:

bulb
bush
cactus
climber
creeper
fern

grass
moss
shrub
succulent
weed
wild flower

Some plants, called annuals,
live for one year only.
A perennial plant lives
year after year.

tree *(noun)*

Types of trees:

ash
banyan
beech
birch
bonsai
cedar
cypress
elm
eucalyptus
fir
gingko
hazel
horse chestnut
juniper
laburnum
larch
linden
magnolia
maple
monkey puzzle
oak
olive
pine
poplar
rowan
spruce
sycamore
willow
yew

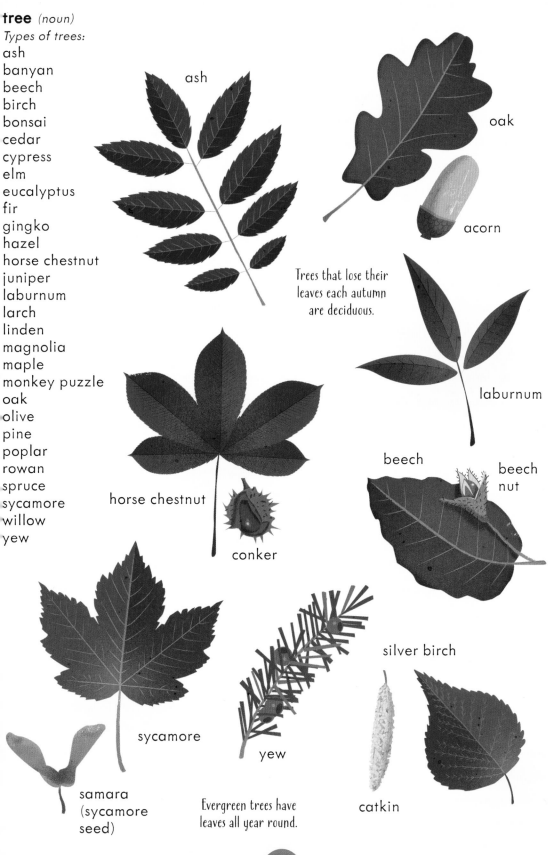

ash

oak

acorn

Trees that lose their leaves each autumn are deciduous.

laburnum

beech

beech nut

horse chestnut

conker

silver birch

sycamore

yew

catkin

samara (sycamore seed)

Evergreen trees have leaves all year round.

21

Animal words

animal *(noun)*
What type of <u>animal</u> is it?

creature
beast

heron

The beavers are busily building their dam.

Types of animals

mammals
aardvark
bat
chimpanzee
deer
hippopotamus
kangaroo
lion
panda
seal
tiger
walrus

birds
blackbird
cockatoo
dove
eagle
flamingo
kingfisher
magpie
ostrich

amphibians
frog
newt
salamander
toad

invertebrates
beetle
dragonfly
earthworm
fly
lobster
scorpion
snail
spider
squid
starfish

reptiles
alligator
crocodile
lizard
python
terrapin
tortoise

fish
angelfish
carp
goldfish
piranha
sea horse
shark
stickleback

beaver

dragonfly

toad

terrapin

A kingfisher catches a fish in its beak.

minnow

A wetland habitat

For some animals, there are different names for the females, males and babies.

animal	female	male	baby
pig	sow	boar	piglet
goat	nanny-goat	billy-goat	kid
deer	doe	stag	fawn
rabbit	doe	buck	kit
elephant	cow	bull	calf
chicken	hen	cockerel	chick
dog	bitch	dog	puppy
cat	cat	tomcat	kitten
duck	duck	drake	duckling
fox	vixen	fox	cub
goose	goose	gander	gosling
kangaroo	doe	buck	joey
lion	lioness	lion	cub
horse	mare	stallion	foal
sheep	ewe	ram	lamb

Groups of animals

a swarm of insects
a herd of deer
a shoal of fish
a brood of chicks
a litter of puppies

a flock of birds
a pack of wolves
a pod of dolphins
a pride of lions
a flock of sheep

a gaggle of geese
an army of frogs
a streak of tigers
a troop of monkeys
a colony of bats

Describing animals

furry *(adjective)*
Orangutans have **furry** coats.

fluffy
fuzzy
hairy
woolly

smooth *(adjective)*
The **smooth**-skinned gecko scuttled up the wall.

silky
velvety

Animals can be...
agile
feathery
lop-eared
poisonous
scaly
shy
sly
speckled
tame
tufted
venomous
vicious
warty
wild

Animals may have...
antlers
beaks
curved claws
fangs
forked tongues
glossy feathers
hooves
horns
paws
stripes
tails
trunks
whiskers

Words for animals that describe what they eat:
- herbivores eat plants and fruit.
- carnivores eat meat.
- omnivores eat everything.

Cats, dogs and other pets

Cat words

cat (noun)
moggie
pussy cat

Types of cats:
Burmese
long-haired cat
Manx cat
short-haired cat
Siamese
tabby
tortoiseshell

miaow (verb)
Did you hear the
cats <u>miaow</u>?

cry
mew

canary

budgerigar

Dog words

dog (noun)
hound
mutt
pooch

Types of dogs:
beagle
bloodhound
boxer
corgi
dachshund
dalmatian
foxhound
golden retriever
greyhound
husky
labrador
mixed-breed
poodle
pug
spaniel
terrier
whippet

bark (verb)
My dogs <u>bark</u> when
the doorbell rings.

woof
growl
yelp
yowl

Other pet words

Other types of pets:
budgerigar
canary
gerbil
goldfish
guinea pig
hamster
mouse
parrot
pony
rabbit
rat
snake

Pets can...
creep
curl up
frisk
frolic
jump
leap
nuzzle
scamper
scratch
slink
sprawl

Pets can live in a...
cage
hutch
kennel
stable
tank

tame (adjective)
Pets are <u>tame</u> animals.

gentle
obedient
well-behaved

Pets can also be...
affectionate
alert
curious
friendly
lazy
loyal
mischievous
playful
sleepy
timid

*Some pets' fur
can be...*
fluffy
glossy
mangy
matted
rough
shaggy
shiny
silky
smooth
soft
wiry

collar

whiskers

paw

Animals
sometimes sit
on their rear
haunches.

munch
munch

24

Insect words

insect (noun)
The <u>insect</u> skittered out of sight.

bug
creepy crawly

honey bee

wasp

hornet

Insects can...
bite
buzz
crawl
dart
flit
flutter
fly
hide
hover
scurry
scuttle
sting

Feelers on an insect's head are also known as antennae.

ladybird

grasshopper

cockroach

housefly

mosquito

Not all insects have wings.

ant

locust

damselfly

beetle

flea

stick insect

become (verb)
Inside its chrysalis a caterpillar will <u>become</u> a butterfly.

change into
develop into
grow into
turn into

moth

Moths change as they grow too.

butterfly

chrysalis

Butterfly life cycle

egg

caterpillar

Every insect has six legs.

praying mantis

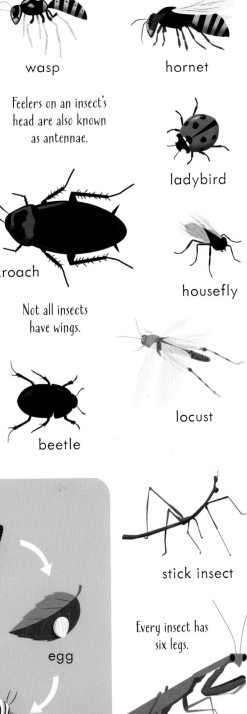

25

Bird sounds

squawk *(verb)*
Birds <u>squawk</u>.

chatter
cheep
chirp
chirrup
cluck
crow
hoot
pipe
screech
sing
trill
twitter
warble
whistle

HOOt HOOt

HOO HOO OOH
twitt twoo

owl

CLUCK
CLUCK
CLUCK

hen

cheep
cheep cheep

chicks

caw
caw

crow

COCK-a
doodle
doo!

cockerel

SQUAWK
pieces of eight
pretty polly

parrot

SCREECH
ee-ee-ee

seagull

quack
quack
quack

duck

HONK
hissssss

COO
COO

pigeon

gobble
gobble
gobble

turkey

goose

26

Noisy words

noise *(noun)*
The chattering crowds made such a <u>noise</u>.

clamour
din
hullabaloo
racket
row
rumpus
sound
tumult

SCREECH

DING DONG

BOOM

SQUEAK

POP

BING

CLOMP

WHAM

CLATTER

CLANG

Sounds

alarm *(noun)*
An <u>alarm</u> whined in the street below.

bell
siren

bang *(noun)*
The firework went off with a loud <u>bang</u>.

boom
explosion
pop

THWACK

THUD

Describing sounds

deep *(adjective)*
The ogre made a <u>deep</u> groan.

low
booming
low-pitched

high *(adjective)*
He blew a <u>high</u> note on his whistle.

high-pitched
piercing
sharp
shrill

loud *(adjective)*
A <u>loud</u> bang resounded.

noisy
booming
ear-splitting
deafening

noisy *(adjective)*
The children were rather <u>noisy</u>.

boisterous
chatty
raucous
rowdy
talkative

quiet *(adjective)*
They spoke in <u>quiet</u> voices so as not to wake the dragon.

hushed
muffled
muted
soft

Noisy things may...

burst *(verb)*
I hate it when balloons <u>burst</u>.

explode
go bang
go pop

ring *(verb)*
The bells <u>ring</u> through the town.

chime
ding
jingle
peal
ping

roar *(verb)*
Did you hear the thunder <u>roar</u>?

boom
rumble

splash *(verb)*
Can you hear the stream <u>splash</u>?

babble
bubble
gurgle

Noisy things may also...
blare
blast
buzz
click
crunch
fizz
sizzle
twang

BANG

crash

Actions

bend (verb)
I must <u>bend</u> down and tie my laces.

crouch
lean
squat
stoop

break (verb)
It's impossible to <u>break</u> this bowl.

chip
crack
damage
destroy
ruin
shatter
smash
wreck

carry (verb)
He can't <u>carry</u> that box.

bear
bring
haul
hold
lug
move

climb (verb)
There's still time to <u>climb</u> the tower.

go up
clamber up
ascend
scale

crawl (verb)
You will have to <u>crawl</u> through that gap.

go on all fours
move on hands
  and knees

creep (verb)
We have to <u>creep</u> past the sleeping dragon.

sneak
slink
inch
tiptoe

cry (verb)
Please try not to <u>cry</u>.

weep
snivel
sob
blub

cut (verb)
I need someone to <u>cut</u> my hair.

clip
snip
trim

die (verb)
They feared their leader might <u>die</u>.

pass away

dive (verb)
She began to <u>dive</u> through the air.

plunge
pitch
plummet
nosedive

fall (verb)
Be careful or you'll <u>fall</u>.

slip
stumble
trip
tumble

find (verb)
What did you <u>find</u> in the shadows?

spot
discover
hit upon
locate
come across
stumble upon

follow (verb)
<u>Follow</u> that car!

chase
go after
pursue
shadow
tail

get off (verb)
We need to <u>get off</u> at the next stop.

alight
disembark
dismount
get out

get on (verb)
The man tried to <u>get on</u> the train.

board
enter
climb aboard

give (verb)
Will you <u>give</u> the money to me?

hand over
offer
present
supply

grip (verb)
You must <u>grip</u> the bars tightly.

clutch
grasp

hug (verb)
The boy had to <u>hug</u> his teddy so he could sleep.

cling to
cuddle
embrace

jump (verb)
Don't <u>jump</u> on the bed.

bounce
leap
spring

kill (verb)
They plotted to <u>kill</u> the king.

murder
assassinate
slay

knock (verb)
Try not to <u>knock</u> your head.

bang
bash
bump

lead *(verb)*
Can you **lead** me to the gallery?

direct
guide

leave *(verb)*
When do you plan to **leave**?

go
depart
make tracks
set off

look *(verb)*
I won't **look**!

watch
gaze
observe
peer
gawp

meet *(verb)*
The soldiers **meet** at noon.

assemble
come together
gather
get together

perform *(verb)*
The actors **perform** on stage.

act
appear

pick up *(verb)*
Can you **pick up** the bread from the bakery?

collect
fetch

poke *(verb)*
Did you **poke** me?

prod
jab
nudge
elbow

pull *(verb)*
They tried to **pull** the rope.

haul
heave
tug
yank

push *(verb)*
Push the clothes into the bag.

press
shove
squeeze
thrust

put *(verb)*
Can you **put** it on the table?

lay
leave
place
plonk
set

reach *(verb)*
When will they **reach** the house?

appear at
arrive at
come to
get to
show up at

run *(verb)*
We have to **run**.

dash
jog
race
rush
scamper
scurry
sprint

shake *(verb)*
The musicians **shake** their maracas.

jiggle
rattle

shut *(verb)*
Don't forget to **shut** the windows.

close
lock
bolt

sit *(verb)*
Let me **sit** here for a moment.

perch
squat

spray *(verb)*
Can you **spray** some water on the roses?

splash
squirt

spread *(verb)*
Let's **spread** the blanket here.

arrange
open out
unroll

squash *(verb)*
You can use your foot to **squash** it.

crush
crumple
flatten

stand *(verb)*
Please **stand** when the teacher comes in.

get up
rise

take *(verb)*
When did he **take** the sweets?

get
grab
receive
seize
snatch

touch *(verb)*
Don't **touch** the material.

feel
finger
handle

twist *(verb)*
Would you help me **twist** the cable?

wind
coil

wave *(verb)*
Don't **wave** your finger at me!

shake
twirl
waggle

Get, go, do...

You might use some verbs, such as 'get', 'go' and 'do', a lot. Try using some of these alternatives instead.

go
(verb)

Let's **go** this way.

walk
hurry
march
ramble
rush
saunter
stride
amble

We have to **go** to New York.

drive
fly
journey
ride
speed
travel
voyage

Where did the monster **go** all of a sudden?

disappear to
vanish to

Where does this track **go**?

end up
lead

Time can **go** slowly when you're bored.

go by
elapse
pass
slip by

The army had to **go** before dusk.

depart
leave
set out

How does the story **go**?

develop
progress
turn out
unfold

The comics **go** on the middle shelf.

belong

get
(verb)

Where did you **get** your top?

buy
acquire
come by
obtain
purchase

Did your dog **get** first prize in the show?

achieve
attain
earn
gain
win

It took us a week to **get** home.

arrive
reach

She went to **get** the drinks.

bring
fetch
retrieve

When will we **get** the answers to the quiz?

be given
hear
receive

The days **get** shorter as winter looms.

become
grow
turn

We tried to **get** him to come but he refused.

coax
convince
force
make
persuade

move (verb)

Try not to **move** until I blow the whistle!

change position
fidget

They had to **move** abroad for work.

emigrate
relocate

They had to **move** carefully past the troll.

advance
journey
proceed

Can you **move** your bike to the shed?

bring
carry
shift
take

Let's **move** before nightfall.

get going
get started
go
make a move
set off

do (verb)

There's so much still to **do**.

accomplish
carry out
finish
undertake

What subject do you **do**?

learn
study

This hotel room will **do**.

be good enough
suffice

Who could **do** the repairs?

arrange
handle
make
manage
organize
prepare
see to
take care of

I hope you'll **do** better next week.

cope
fare
get on
manage
perform

The boy couldn't **do** the puzzle.

answer
crack
figure out
solve
work out

want (verb)

"What do you **want**?" asked the genie.

crave
desire
dream of
fancy
long for
yearn for
wish for

try (verb)

I'll **try** to run faster next time.

aim
attempt

need (verb)

The task will **need** more time if it's to be done properly.

call for
depend on
require

let (verb)

I will **let** you just this once.

allow
permit

have to (verb)

You **have to** try new things.

must
ought to
need to

Instead of said

answered *(verb)*
"I don't think so,"
Dylan **answered**.

replied
responded

asked *(verb)*
"Can I have some more?"
asked Oliver.

begged
demanded
pleaded
questioned

confessed *(verb)*
"It was me!" **confessed** Asha.

admitted
blurted out
owned up

whispered *(verb)*
"Did you hear that?"
whispered Ella.

mumbled
murmured
muttered

thought *(verb)*
"Should I stay?"
thought Zac.

brooded
pondered
wondered

shouted *(verb)*
"Don't!" **shouted**
Maisie.

screamed
bellowed

ordered
barked
snapped
yelled

BOO HOO

WAAAAAH

cried *(verb)*
"Help!" **cried** Archie.

bawled
blubbed
gulped
howled

shrieked
sobbed
squealed
wept
whimpered

ha ha HO HO

laughed *(verb)*
"That's ridiculous,"
laughed Ali.

chortled
chuckled

giggled
sniggered
tittered

moaned *(verb)*
"Oh no," **moaned** Ruth.

complained
grumbled
sighed
whined
whinged

spoke *(verb)*
"Set her free!" **spoke**
the queen.

announced
declared
stated

quickly *(adverb)*
"Come on!" Jimmy
said **quickly**.

hastily
hurriedly
rushedly
swiftly

slowly *(adverb)*
"I'm tired," Freya
said **slowly**.

haltingly
lazily
leisurely
sluggishly

loudly *(adverb)*
"Don't!" Finn
said **loudly**.

noisily
powerfully
thunderingly

quietly *(adverb)*
"Keep still," Kate
said **quietly**.

faintly
gently
softly

Weather words

What's the weather like?

cloudy *(adjective)*
dull
grey
overcast

cold *(adjective)*
chilly
cool
bitter
bracing
nippy

foggy *(adjective)*
misty
hazy
murky

hot *(adjective)*
balmy
boiling
scorching
sweltering
tropical
warm

humid *(adjective)*
clammy
close
muggy
sultry

rainy *(adjective)*
damp
drizzly
pouring
showery
spitting
wet

stormy *(adjective)*
thundery

sunny *(adjective)*
bright
clear
cloudless
fine

windy *(adjective)*
blustery
breezy

Writing about the weather

The sun may...
shine
glare

Types of hot weather:
drought
heatwave

Rain may...
pour
teem
lash
pelt

Types of wet weather:
downpour
rain shower
sleet

Snow may...
drift
swirl
settle

Wind may...
batter
blast
blow
howl
roar

Types of windy weather:
breeze
gust
gale
tornado
whirlwind

Thunder may...
boom
crash
rumble

Types of stormy weather:
blizzard
hail
snowstorm
thunderstorm

Weather map symbols

sunny   cloudy   sunny intervals

light rain   sunshine and showers   snow

sleet   hail   thunder

12

Temperature is measured in degrees Celsius (°C) or degrees Fahrenheit (°F).

9

Wind speed and direction

33

Night words

night *(noun)*
The fox hunted in the <u>night</u>.

darkness
hours of darkness
night-time
small hours

Animals that stay awake at night are nocturnal.

owl

bat

fireflies

fox

raccoon

Describing night

dark *(adjective)*
An owl flew across a <u>dark</u> sky.

dusky
gloomy
inky
moonless
pitch-black
shadowy
starless

quiet *(adjective)*
The night was long and <u>quiet</u>.

silent
hushed
still

Night can also be...
moonlit
starry

Night-time things

bed *(noun)*
Types of bed:
air
bunk
cot
double
four-poster
futon
king-sized
sofa

dream *(noun)*
I had a strange <u>dream</u> last night.

bad dream
nightmare

teddy *(noun)*
The name of my <u>teddy</u> is Jumbo.

soft toy
stuffed animal
teddy bear

She gazed keenly through her telescope at the stars in the night sky.

skylight

crescent moon

moths

streetlight

cat

The hedgehog was searching for slugs to gobble.

hedgehog

Describing people at night

afraid (adjective)
I'm <u>afraid</u> of the dark.

frightened
scared
terrified
petrified

asleep (adjective)
The baby was <u>asleep</u>.

fast asleep
napping
sleeping

awake (adjective)
It was midnight,
but he was still <u>awake</u>.

wide-awake

tired (adjective)
The woman was so <u>tired</u>,
she fell straight to sleep.

sleepy
exhausted
drowsy
weary
worn out

Things people do at night

lie (verb)
The lazy boy wanted
to <u>lie</u> in bed all day.

loll
lounge
recline
sprawl

rest (verb)
It's late and I
must <u>rest</u>.

have a rest
relax
take a nap

sleep (verb)
His uncle will <u>sleep</u>
through anything.

doze
slumber
snooze

wake up (verb)
The bright light made
them <u>wake up</u>.

get up
stir
wake

Story starters

The clock struck midnight as Fox began his nightly prowl...

Every house in the town was shrouded in darkness, except for one where a lamp still glowed...

Time words

time *(noun)*
The family went away for a long **time**.
period
spell
while

time *(verb)*
Can you **time** my swim please?
measure

clock *(noun)*
Types of clock:
alarm clock
grandfather clock
hourglass

analogue clock

buckle

strap

pocketwatch

watch

stopwatch

06:30
digital clock

When?

day *(noun)*
Bats sleep during the **day**.
daylight
daytime

evening *(noun)*
Clouds gathered as **evening** approached.
dusk
sunset
twilight

finally *(adverb)*
Finally the ship arrived.
at last
eventually
in the end

immediately *(adverb)*
Let's leave **immediately**.
at once
now
promptly
right now
straightaway

moment *(noun)*
The guests will arrive in a **moment**.
instant
little while
second

morning *(noun)*
Is it **morning** yet?
dawn
sunrise

In what order?

first *(adverb)*
First the teacher stood up.
firstly
first of all

last *(adverb)*
The band played **last**.
at the end
last of all
lastly

next *(adverb)*
Who arrived **next**?
after that
afterwards
later
then

How often?

always *(adverb)*
That man is **always** on time.
consistently
forever
unfailingly

often *(adverb)*
That absent-minded girl is **often** late.
frequently
generally
regularly
usually

sometimes *(adverb)*
Everyone forgets **sometimes**.
occasionally
on occasion

How far? How much?

about *(adverb)*
The town is <u>about</u> a mile away.

approximately
around
nearly
roughly

exactly *(adverb)*
The station is <u>exactly</u> a mile away.

precisely

far *(adverb)*
The ship sailed <u>far</u>.

a long way
for miles

nearly *(adverb)*
An elephant weighs <u>nearly</u> as much as 60 people.

almost
just about

quite *(adverb)*
This suitcase is <u>quite</u> heavy.

fairly
rather
reasonably
somewhat

Where?

back *(noun)*
We always sit at the <u>back</u> of the bus.

end
far end
rear

faraway
(adjective)
The captain explored <u>faraway</u> lands.

distant
farflung
remote

front *(noun)*
We reached the <u>front</u> of the queue.

head
start

near *(preposition)*
I want to live <u>near</u> the sea.

close to
next to
not far from

opposite
(preposition)
The boxer sat <u>opposite</u> his rival.

across from

place *(noun)*
Let's pitch the tent in a <u>place</u> that is safe and dry.

location
position
spot

measurements *(noun)*
Write down the room's <u>measurements</u>.

dimensions
length   height
size

width

Distance is measured in...
millimetres (mm)
centimetres (cm)
inches (in)
feet (ft)
yards (yd)
metres (m)
kilometres (km)
miles (mi)

Weight is measured in...
grams (g)
ounces (oz)
pounds (lb)
kilograms (kg)
stones (st)

The seasons

blossom

nest

Spring

babies *(noun)*
Lots of animals have their <u>babies</u>.

young

build *(verb)*
Some birds <u>build</u> nests.

make
construct
put together

grow *(verb)*
Many plants start to <u>grow</u>.

get bigger
develop
shoot up

melt *(verb)*
The snow begins to <u>melt</u> as it gets warmer.

defrost
soften
thaw

The first tulips open as the last daffodils are still in bloom.

tulips   daffodils

Summer

increase *(verb)*
The days <u>increase</u> in length.

get longer
expand
draw out

open *(verb)*
Many flowers start to <u>open</u>.

bloom
burst open

play *(verb)*
Children <u>play</u> outside.

have fun
play games

shrivel *(verb)*
Plants may <u>shrivel</u> in the heat.

droop
wilt
wither

parasol

picnic hamper

deck chair

Autumn

decrease *(verb)*
The hours of daylight <u>decrease</u>.

get shorter
fall
dwindle

hang *(verb)*
The old branches <u>hang</u> low.

droop
bow
sag

fall *(verb)*
Leaves <u>fall</u> from the trees.

flutter down
swirl
tumble

mist *(noun)*
There's a <u>mist</u> in the air.

fog
haze

conkers

squirrel

toadstool

acorns

Snowflakes tumble gently through the air.

robin

icicle

snowman

snowdrift

Winter

bear *(verb)*
Animals have to <u>bear</u> the cold weather.

put up with
suffer

cold *(adjective)*
In some places it gets very <u>cold</u>.

chilly
bracing
crisp
fresh
frosty
icy
nippy

cover *(verb)*
Snow may <u>cover</u> the ground.

blanket
carpet
hide
lie on

hard *(adjective)*
The ground freezes <u>hard</u>.

firm
rigid
solid

In the town

town (noun)
Thousands of people live in the <u>town</u>.

city
metropolis

A town may be...
bustling
crowded
lively
overwhelming
throbbing

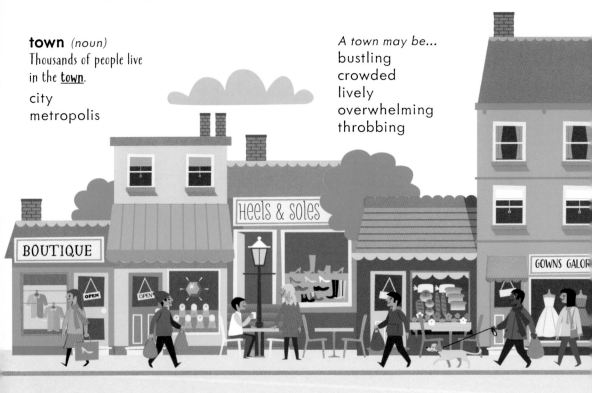

Sights and places

area (noun)
This part is a nice <u>area</u>.

place
district

restaurant (noun)
Which <u>restaurant</u> shall we go to?

café
brasserie
bistro
pizzeria

street (noun)
Meet me at the end of the <u>street</u>!

avenue
boulevard
crescent
cul-de-sac
lane
road

Other sights and places:
art gallery
bridge
cinema
fountain
gym
hotel
ice rink
library
museum
opera house
park
river
shopping centre
square
station
subway
swimming pool
theatre
town square

Shopping

buy (verb)
Where did you <u>buy</u> those clothes?

get
pay for
purchase

market (noun)
There are lots of stalls at the <u>market</u>.

bazaar
fair
flea market
marketplace

money (noun)
Can you lend me some <u>money</u> to buy the book?

cash
coins

queue (noun)
The customers waited in a <u>queue</u> to be served.

line

shop (noun)
Where's the nearest <u>shop</u>, please?

boutique
corner shop
megastore
store
supermarket

spend (verb)
How much money did you <u>spend</u>?

pay
splurge

In the countryside

countryside *(noun)*
Let's go for a walk in the <u>countryside</u>.

country
wilds

Things you might see

bog *(noun)*
The ground is very wet near the <u>bog</u>.

marsh
fen
swamp
wetlands

hill *(noun)*
Did you climb to the top of the <u>hill</u>?

hillside
mound

hole *(noun)*
The rambler twisted his ankle in the <u>hole</u>.

dip
hollow
pit
trench

hut *(noun)*
The woman lived in a lonely <u>hut</u> in the woods.

cabin
shack
shed
shelter

litter *(noun)*
They tidied up their <u>litter</u> after the picnic.

rubbish
waste

notice *(noun)*
The <u>notice</u> says the field is flooded.

sign
poster

path *(noun)*
You must take the <u>path</u> round the lake.

lane
pathway
track
trail

post *(noun)*
Stay to the left of that <u>post</u>!

pillar
pole
stake

Other things:
orchard
windmill

River words

river *(noun)*
We had to wade through the <u>river</u>.

stream
creek
brook
rivulet

Rivers may...
babble
eddy
gush
meander
trickle

Parts of a river:
estuary (mouth
  of a river)
riverbank
source
waterfall
weir

Describing the countryside

calm *(adjective)*
It's so <u>calm</u> in the country.

peaceful
quiet
serene
tranquil

clean *(adjective)*
The water in the lake was ever so <u>clean</u>.

clear
fresh
pure
unpolluted

Farm words

farm *(noun)*
Types of farm:
arable farm (grows crops)
dairy farm (keeps cows)
livestock farm (keeps animals)
smallholding (a very small farm)

orchard

farmhouse

MOO

feeder

stable

pail
(bucket)

CLIP
CLOP

vegetable
patch

scarecrow

cockerel

coop

hens

sty

The ground in the pigs' pen was
squelchy and muddy.

squeal

duck pond

trough

42

CHUG
CHUG

combine
harvester

field *(noun)*
The farmer is in the <u>field</u>.
meadow
paddock
pasture
plain

barn

tractor

hay bale

WOOF

flock of
sheep

The sheepdog
chased the sheep
through the yard.

baaa

OINK

baaa

Writing about farms

even *(adjective)*
He raked the soil until
it was <u>even</u>.
flat
level
smooth

keep *(verb)*
The farmers <u>keep</u> ducks
on their farm.
care for
have
look after
tend

row *(noun)*
She planted a <u>row</u> of
strawberry plants.
line

Farms grow...
barley
fruit
maize
oats
oilseed rape
sunflowers
vegetables
wheat

Describing farm animals

Types of cows:
Friesian
Hereford
Jersey

Types of pigs:
Mangalitza
Tamworth
Vietnamese
  pot-bellied

Types of horses:
carthorse
colt (young male)
filly (young female)

Horses may...
canter
gallop
jump
prance

Colours of horses:
bay (brown)
chestnut
dapple-grey
piebald (spotty)

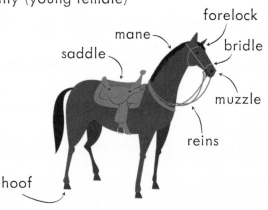

forelock
mane
bridle
saddle
muzzle
reins
hoof

Seaside words

Places at the seaside

beach (noun)
Can we go to the <u>beach</u> today?

seashore
shore

port (noun)
Boats bobbed up and down in the <u>port</u>.

dock
harbour
marina

Other seaside places:
caravan site
cliffs
funfair
guesthouse
hotel
pier
promenade
souvenir shop

Describing the seaside

busy (adjective)
The beach was <u>busy</u> with people.

crowded
heaving
packed

Beaches can be...
golden
muddy
pebbly
sandy
shingly
stony
windswept

Cliffs can be...
chalky
craggy
rocky

Things you might find on the beach:
beach ball
beach hut
bucket and spade
deck chair
parasol
sandcastle
windbreak

Seaside creatures

Rockpool creatures:
barnacle
hermit crab
sea anemone
sea urchin
shrimp
starfish

Seaside birds:
cormorant
fulmar
guillemot
gull
kittiwake
puffin

Things to do at the seaside

dip (verb)
We dared to <u>dip</u> our toes in the icy sea.

dunk
lower
plunge

swim (verb)
I want to <u>swim</u> in the sea.

go for a swim
go swimming
take a dip

Swimming strokes:
back stroke
breast stroke
butterfly
doggy paddle
front crawl

Other things to do:
crab fishing
explore rockpools
paddle
sail
snorkel
sunbathe
surf

Things you might eat
candyfloss
fish
ice cream
seafood

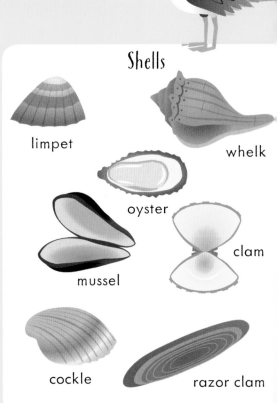

Shells

limpet
whelk
oyster
clam
mussel
cockle
razor clam

promenade

wave

dinghy

The tide was coming in.

lighthouse

lifeguard

lilo

windsurfer

yacht

kitesurfer

sandcastle

rockpools

Jungle words

jungle (noun)
The <u>jungle</u> is home to lots of animals.

rainforest
tropical forest

sloth

snake

SSSSSSSS

toucan

butterfly

chameleon

swamp

crocodile

snap
snap

Describing jungles

dark (adjective)
It can be <u>dark</u> in a jungle.

gloomy
shady
shadowy

wet (adjective)
Jungles can be very <u>wet</u> places.

damp
dank
humid
moist
muggy

Writing about jungle plants

dangle (verb)
Vines <u>dangle</u> from the branches.

hang down
trail

thick (adjective)
Jungle plants are <u>thick</u> with leaves.

bushy
dense
leafy
lush
teeming

wind (verb)
Climbing plants <u>wind</u> around tree trunks.

twist
coil
loop
snake
wrap

Jungle plants:
palms
bamboo
lianas

Jungle explorers

climb (verb)
Explorers <u>climb</u> over rocks.

clamber
scramble

search (verb)
They <u>search</u> for things to eat.

hunt
look
seek
forage

monkey

oo-oo-oo

parrot

canopy
(top layer
of a jungle)

vine

explorer

tree
frog

gorilla

RAAAAAA

jaguar

orchid

ants

forest floor

fern

Things jungle animals do

attack *(verb)*
Jaguars <u>attack</u> their prey.
ambush
pounce on
strike at

chase *(verb)*
Tigers <u>chase</u> other animals.
hunt
pursue
stalk
track

creep *(verb)*
Crocodiles <u>creep</u> along the riverbank.
crawl
inch
scrabble

fly *(verb)*
Insects <u>fly</u> up high.
flit
flutter
hover

hide *(verb)*
Creatures <u>hide</u> in the shadows.
lie low
lurk
prowl
skulk

jump *(verb)*
Monkeys <u>jump</u> between trees.
leap
swing

rush *(verb)*
Animals <u>rush</u> to escape.
dart
dash
race
scuttle

wriggle *(verb)*
Snakes <u>wriggle</u> along branches.
slither
slink
squirm
zigzag

In the mountains

cable car

mountain rescue

snow-capped mountains

avalanche

slope

chalet

snowboard

slalom

climbers

foot (bottom of a mountain)

dog sled

fir trees

bear

wolf

ripple

SPLOSH

alpine lake

reflection

dangerous
(adjective)
It was a <u>dangerous</u> mountain to climb.

hazardous
precarious
risky
treacherous

high *(adjective)*
The <u>high</u> mountain touched the clouds.

lofty
soaring
towering

Mountains can also be...
craggy
forest-fringed
misty
rocky
rugged
sheer

Things to do in the mountains:
climb
hike
ski
snowboard
toboggan
trek

In the desert

camel

sand dune

prickly pear

cactus

palm tree

Animals seek out the oasis for water to drink.

vulture

oasis/water hole

skull

desert fox

A snake slithers noiselessly from behind a rock.

scorpion

snake

bright *(adjective)*
A **bright** sun shone in the sky.

blazing
dazzling
fiery
glaring
scorching

dry *(adjective)*
The desert is a **dry** place.

arid
bone dry
dusty
parched
sandy

hot *(adjective)*
It's **hot** at midday.

boiling hot
sweltering
searing
blistering

spiky *(adjective)*
He pricked his thumb on a **spiky** cactus.

spiny
prickly
thorny

Under the sea

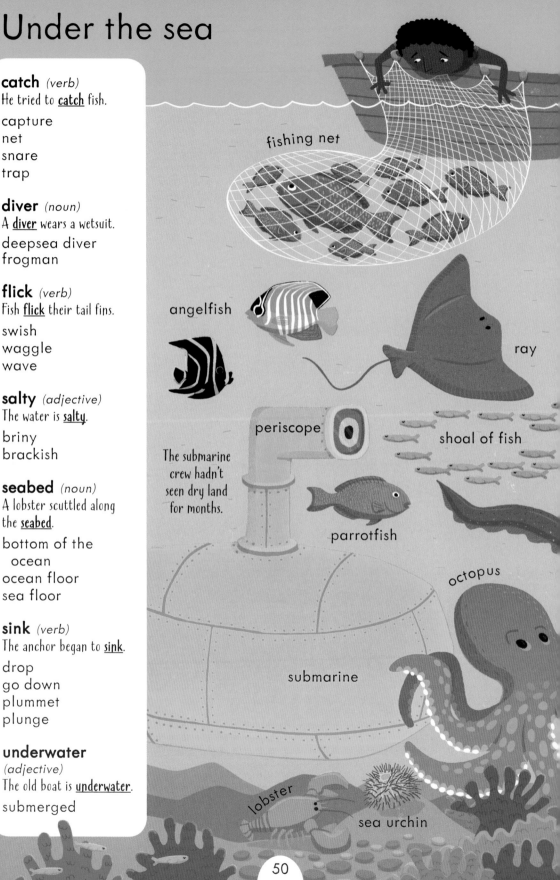

catch *(verb)*
He tried to <u>catch</u> fish.

capture
net
snare
trap

diver *(noun)*
A <u>diver</u> wears a wetsuit.

deepsea diver
frogman

flick *(verb)*
Fish <u>flick</u> their tail fins.

swish
waggle
wave

salty *(adjective)*
The water is <u>salty</u>.

briny
brackish

seabed *(noun)*
A lobster scuttled along the <u>seabed</u>.

bottom of the
   ocean
ocean floor
sea floor

sink *(verb)*
The anchor began to <u>sink</u>.

drop
go down
plummet
plunge

underwater
(adjective)
The old boat is <u>underwater</u>.

submerged

fishing net

angelfish

ray

periscope

shoal of fish

The submarine
crew hadn't
seen dry land
for months.

parrotfish

octopus

submarine

lobster

sea urchin

50

Above the water all is calm, but in the ocean below a throng of sea creatures swim to and fro.

fin/flipper

oxygen tank

diver

wetsuit

jellyfish

seahorse

A menacing shark stalked its prey.

squid

The spiky fish filled its body with water to puff itself up.

shark

electric eel

kelp

pufferfish

clown fish

sea turtle

pincer

crab

tentacle

anchor

wreck

coral

Story endings

By the time the cloud of sand had cleared, the giant squid had disappeared.

Desperate for air, she snatched the pearl from the clam and swam to the surface.

Would anyone ever explore this city under the sea again?

Under the ground

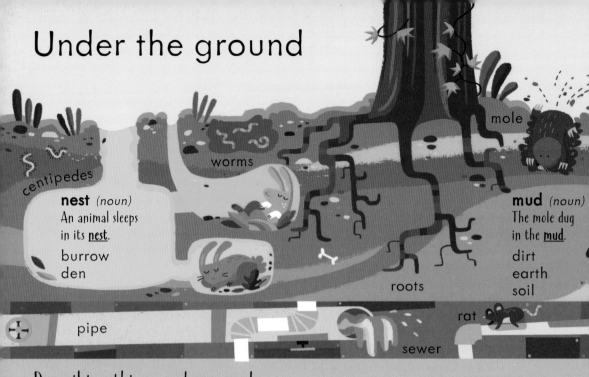

mole

worms

centipedes

nest *(noun)*
An animal sleeps in its <u>nest</u>.
burrow
den

mud *(noun)*
The mole dug in the <u>mud</u>.
dirt
earth
soil

roots

pipe

rat

sewer

Describing things underground

deep *(adjective)*
The <u>deep</u> pit went on and on.
bottomless
cavernous
gaping

hard *(adjective)*
A machine cut through the <u>hard</u> earth.
firm
solid
tough

old *(adjective)*
There are <u>old</u> remains deep underground.
ancient
aged
prehistoric

smelly *(adjective)*
It was pitch black in the <u>smelly</u>, clammy sewer.
stinking
pongy
reeking
fetid

cables

underground train

tracks

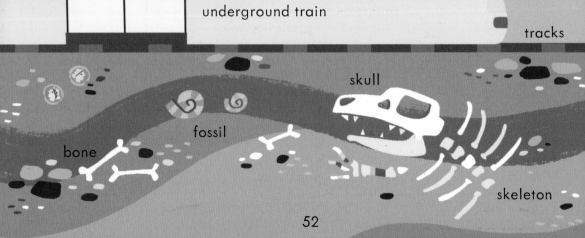

skull

fossil

bone

skeleton

In the air

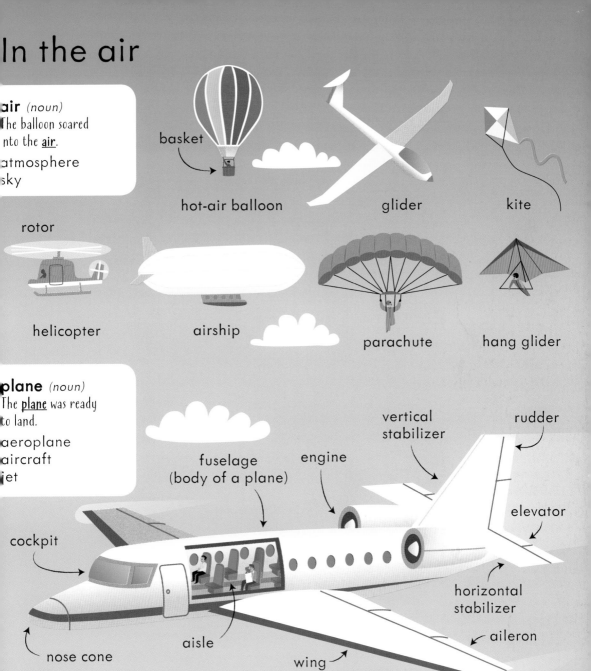

air *(noun)*
The balloon soared into the **air**.

atmosphere
sky

basket

hot-air balloon

glider

kite

rotor

helicopter

airship

parachute

hang glider

plane *(noun)*
The **plane** was ready to land.

aeroplane
aircraft
jet

cockpit

nose cone

aisle

wing

fuselage
(body of a plane)

engine

vertical stabilizer

rudder

elevator

horizontal stabilizer

aileron

control *(verb)*
Two pilots **control** the plane.

fly
navigate
operate
pilot

glide *(verb)*
See how they **glide** through the air.

drift
float
hover
sail

rise *(verb)*
The plane will steadily **rise**.

go up
climb
ascend
soar
rocket

type *(noun)*
Every **type** of aircraft was at the airshow.

kind
sort
variety

Boat words

boat (noun)
They sailed the **boat** around the island.

ship
craft
vessel

Types of boat:
aircraft carrier
barge
battleship
canoe
catamaran
container ship
cruise liner
dinghy
ferry
fishing boat
galleon
gondola
hovercraft
kayak
lifeboat
motorboat
narrow boat
punt
raft
rowing boat
sailing boat
speedboat
tanker
trawler
tug
yacht

People out on deck watched whales dive and splash.

bridge

ship's wheel

bow (front of a boat)

lifejackets

anchor

The two-hulled catamaran sailed at speed.

A container ship carried its heavy cargo across the ocean.

Boats can...
bob up and
  down
capsize
cruise
dock
drift
float
glide
heave
plough through
  the water
rock from side
  to side
sail
set sail
speed
steam ahead

funnel

lifeboats

porthole

hull (body of a boat)

stern (back of a boat)

buoy

propeller

yacht

rudder

keel

A motorboat zipped through the water leaving a trail of foam.

oar

The rower held a steady path through the water.

55

On the road

road *(noun)*
street
lane
avenue
motorway
route
track

car *(noun)*
automobile
motor
vehicle

fresh

HONK

drive *(verb)*
It's hard to **drive** this truck.
manoeuvre
operate
steer

beep beep

lorry *(noun)*
truck
juggernaut

pedestrian
crossing

TOOT

traffic jam *(noun)*
They're stuck in a **traffic jam**.
bottleneck
gridlock
hold up

hoot

taxi

road sign

traffic
light

caravan

start *(verb)*
The driver tried to **start** the engine.
activate
fire up
switch on
turn on

roundabout

stop *(verb)*
They had to **stop** suddenly.
brake
slow down
halt
decelerate

petrol
station

FUEL

speed *(verb)*
The motorbikes **speed** around the corner.
accelerate
tear
zip
zoom

vroom

vroom

fast *(adjective)*
She drove a **fast** car.
quick
speedy
swift
powerful

siren

POLICE

bicycle

bridge

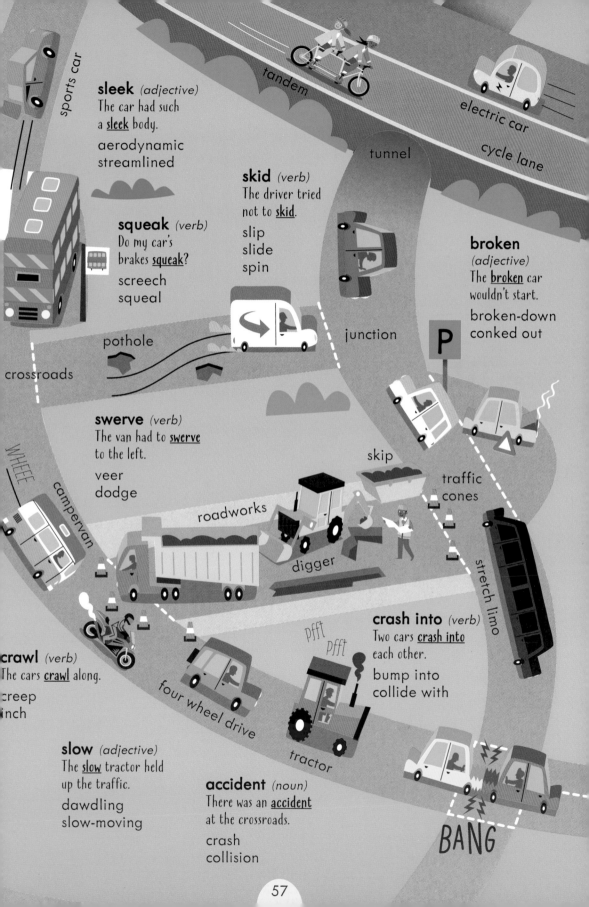

sports car

tandem

electric car

cycle lane

tunnel

sleek (adjective)
The car had such a <u>sleek</u> body.
aerodynamic
streamlined

skid (verb)
The driver tried not to <u>skid</u>.
slip
slide
spin

broken (adjective)
The <u>broken</u> car wouldn't start.
broken-down
conked out

squeak (verb)
Do my car's brakes <u>squeak</u>?
screech
squeal

pothole

junction

crossroads

P

swerve (verb)
The van had to <u>swerve</u> to the left.
veer
dodge

skip

traffic cones

WHEEE

campervan

roadworks

digger

stretch limo

crash into (verb)
Two cars <u>crash into</u> each other.
bump into
collide with

pfft pfft

crawl (verb)
The cars <u>crawl</u> along.
creep
inch

four wheel drive

tractor

slow (adjective)
The <u>slow</u> tractor held up the traffic.
dawdling
slow-moving

accident (noun)
There was an <u>accident</u> at the crossroads.
crash
collision

BANG

Travel words

departure board

train *(noun)*
engine
locomotive

Types of train:
diesel train
electric train
freight train
high-speed train
maglev
monorail
steam train
underground train

Trains...
clank
depart
grind to a halt
hurtle
pull into a station
trundle
whistle

Fwee
Fwee

The guard blows two short blasts on his whistle.

abroad *(adverb)*
The family often go <u>abroad</u> all summer.

overseas

cancel *(verb)*
They had to <u>cancel</u> all the trains because of the deep snow.

call off
scrap

country *(noun)*
The boat sailed from one <u>country</u> to another.

land

delay *(verb)*
The airline had to <u>delay</u> the flight.

postpone
suspend

journey *(noun)*
Where did your <u>journey</u> take you?

excursion
expedition
tour
travels
trek
trip
voyage

late *(adjective)*
The driver was <u>late</u>.

behind schedule
delayed
not on time

luggage *(noun)*
The man put his <u>luggage</u> in the compartment.

bag
case
baggage
rucksack
suitcase
wheelie bag

prepare *(verb)*
Did you <u>prepare</u> for the trip?

get ready
make plans
plan
train

ready *(adjective)*
Everything was <u>ready</u> for the journey.

arranged
organized
prepared
set up

Passengers sit patiently in the carriage waiting for the train to depart.

tickets

luggage trolley

People stride up
and down the platform.

squeeze *(verb)*
She tried to <u>squeeze</u>
a second jumper
into her bag.

cram
pack
stuff

travel *(verb)*
My brother loves
to <u>travel</u>.

go abroad
see the world
tour

*While travelling you
may feel...*
excited
fidgety
jet-lagged
nervous
seasick
travel-sick

Items to pack:
book
map
passport
phrase book
snacks
ticket

Bike words

bike *(noun)*
bicycle
cycle

Types of bike:
folding bike
mountain bike
road bike
tandem
tricycle
unicycle

Story starter
and ending

"Your prize is a plane
ticket to anywhere in
the world..."

Unpacking their
cases they agreed it
couldn't have been
a better trip.

Feeling ill

behave (verb)
His fever made the man <u>behave</u> oddly.

act

catch (verb)
How did the patient <u>catch</u> a cold?

get
develop
contract
pick up

cut (verb)
When did the chef <u>cut</u> her finger?

graze
nick
sever
slash

different (adjective)
The patient has <u>different</u> symptoms.

mixed
various

dizzy (adjective)
The girl felt <u>dizzy</u>.

faint
light-headed
shaky
wobbly
woozy

doctor (noun)
Can I see a <u>doctor</u>?

medic
physician

Types of doctor:
consultant
GP (general
  practitioner)
surgeon

health (noun)
Walking is good for your <u>health</u>.

fitness
wellbeing

hurt (verb)
How did you <u>hurt</u> your leg?

harm
injure
wound

ill (adjective)
Are you still <u>ill</u>?

unwell
poorly
out of sorts

illness (noun)
The doctor diagnosed her <u>illness</u>.

sickness
bug
disease
infection
ailment
virus

itch (verb)
The rash made his skin <u>itch</u>.

prickle
tingle

knock (verb)
What did you <u>knock</u> your knee on?

bang
bump
hit
strike

look after (verb)
They'll <u>look after</u> you.

care for
take care of
treat

loose (adjective)
The boy had a <u>loose</u> front tooth.

wobbly

lump (noun)
There's a strange <u>lump</u> on his arm.

bump
bulge
swelling

medicine (noun)
The doctor prescribed this <u>medicine</u>.

drug
medication
remedy

Types of medicine:
antibiotic
cream
injection
lotion
ointment
painkiller
pill
spray
tablet

x-ray

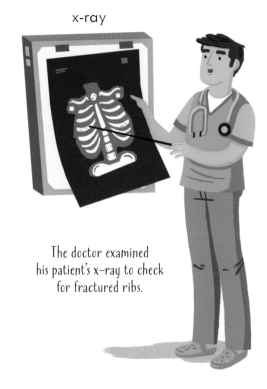

The doctor examined his patient's x-ray to check for fractured ribs.

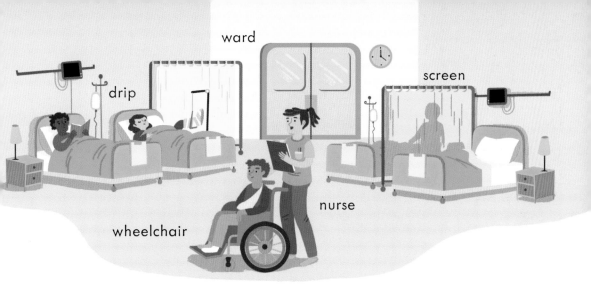

ward

drip

screen

nurse

wheelchair

pain *(noun)*
She felt a slight **pain** in her back.

ache
cramp
discomfort
soreness
twinge

pale *(adjective)*
His skin looks **pale**.

pasty
ashen
sickly

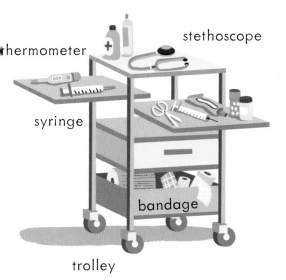

stethoscope

thermometer

syringe

bandage

trolley

problem *(noun)*
What is the **problem**?

difficulty
trouble
predicament

recover *(verb)*
You will **recover** in a week or so.

get better
get well
heal
improve
recuperate

serious *(adjective)*
The old man had a **serious** illness.

critical
grave
major

sick *(adjective)*
I felt **sick** on the train.

unwell
ill
nauseous
queasy
bilious

soothe *(verb)*
The nurse tried to **soothe** his patient.

calm
comfort
reassure

sore *(adjective)*
The young woman's leg was really **sore**.

aching
bruised
hurting
painful
tender

weak *(adjective)*
My great uncle feels **weak** after his operation.

delicate
feeble
frail

well *(adjective)*
When will the patient be **well** again?

fit
healthy
in good health

wheeze *(verb)*
She suddenly started to **wheeze**.

breathe heavily
gasp
pant

worry *(verb)*
You'll feel better if you don't **worry**.

fret
fuss
get worked up

Buildings

building *(noun)*
house
block of flats

Types of buildings:
factory
garage
hotel
mill
museum
office
palace
power station
prison
skyscraper
station
surgery
theatre
tower block

Describing buildings

Buildings can be made of...
brick
concrete
glass
marble
steel
stone
timber

Buildings can be...
crumbling
futuristic
gleaming
imposing
lofty
ornate
towering

Glistening towers of glass and steel stood shoulder to shoulder along the horizon.

helipad

spire

Each level of a building is known as a storey.

tower

roof garden

dome

belfry

balcony

Building things

block *(noun)*
Each <u>block</u> was
made of stone.

brick
slab

build *(verb)*
It took ten years
to <u>build</u> the castle.

construct
erect
put up

crack *(noun)*
There was a <u>crack</u>
in the wall.

gap
hole

dig *(verb)*
The builders <u>dig</u> a huge
hole for the foundations.

excavate

join *(verb)*
The plumbers <u>join</u> the
pipes together.

attach
connect
fasten
fix

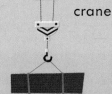

crane

cabin

lump *(noun)*
He added the concrete
in a <u>lump</u>.

blob
dollop
splodge

make *(verb)*
How did they <u>make</u>
the plaster?

form
shape
mould

pile *(noun)*
They put the
bags in a <u>pile</u>.

heap
mound
stack

plan *(noun)*
They studied the
<u>plan</u> before they
began building.

design
diagram
drawing
sketch

pulley

cut *(verb)*
They had to <u>cut</u> the
planks in half.

chop
divide
saw

layer *(noun)*
The walls need
another <u>layer</u>
of paint.

coat
covering

piece *(noun)*
They built the tower
<u>piece</u> by <u>piece</u>.

bit
part
section

size *(noun)*
She cut the boards
to the right <u>size</u>.

measurements
dimensions
height
length
breadth
width

scaffolding

bricklayer

concrete mixer

bulldozer

fork lift truck

Around the house

house *(noun)*
home
abode
dwelling

Types of house:
bungalow
cabin
cottage
detached house
mansion
semi-detached
 house
terraced house
villa

*Other places
where people live:*
apartment
bedsit
caravan
flat
houseboat
maisonette
motor home

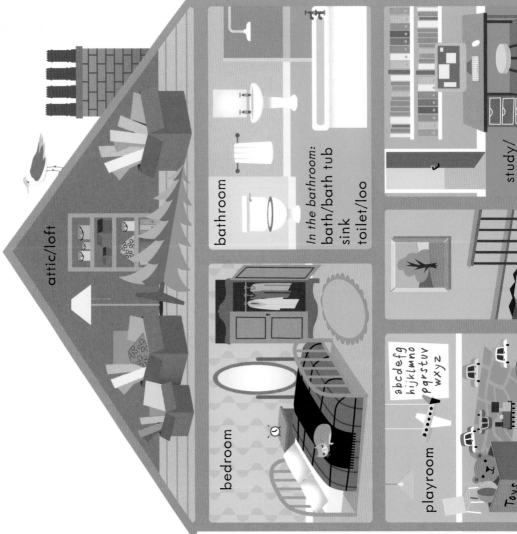

attic/loft

bedroom

bathroom

In the bathroom:
bath/bath tub
sink
toilet/loo

playroom

Toys

study/
...

Inside a house

chair *(noun)*
seat

Types of chair:
armchair
bench
dining chair
rocking chair
stool

Types of furniture:
bookcase
cabinet
coffee table
desk
dining table
shelf
wardrobe

On the floors:
carpet
wooden flooring
rugs
tiles

On the walls:
paint
tiles
wallpaper
wood panelling

Things people do inside a house

clean (verb)
We need to **clean** every room.

tidy
wash
polish
scrub
spring-clean
sweep
brush
vacuum
dust
wipe

close (verb)
Can you **close** the curtains, please?

shut
pull
draw

decorate (verb)
I want to **decorate** the walls.

paint
wallpaper

dining room

sitting room/living room/lounge

kitchen

In the kitchen:
cooker
dishwasher
hob
refrigerator
sink
washing machine
tumble dryer

hall

basement/cellar

Describing a house

chilly (adjective)
It was **chilly** in their flat.

cold
airy
draughty

cosy (adjective)
The cottage is **cosy**.

comfortable
comfy
snug
warm

mess (noun)
Tidy up the **mess**!

clutter
jumble

messy (adjective)
Her bungalow was always **messy**.

dusty
untidy

tidy (adjective)
The boy kept his room **tidy**.

clean
neat
spick-and-span
uncluttered

Clothes words

clothes *(noun)*
attire
clothing
costume
outfit

bag *(noun)*
backpack
handbag
rucksack
satchel
shoulder bag

coat *(noun)*
anorak
cagoule
duffle coat
parka
raincoat
trench coat

dress *(noun)*
ball gown
cocktail dress
frock
mini dress
prom dress
sari
sun dress
wedding dress

hat *(noun)*
baseball cap
beanie
beret
bobble hat
bowler hat
cap
deerstalker
fez
sombrero
top hat

jacket *(noun)*
blazer
bomber jacket
denim jacket
tuxedo

shoes *(noun)*
ankle boots
ballet pumps
baseball boots
boots
cowboy boots
espadrilles
heels
sandals
slippers
stilettos
trainers
walking boots
wellingtons

skirt *(noun)*
kilt
miniskirt

suit *(noun)*
boiler suit
lounge suit
three-piece suit
tracksuit
trouser suit

top *(noun)*
blouse
cardigan
fleece
jumper
polo shirt
pullover
sweatshirt
tanktop
T-shirt
vest

trousers *(noun)*
chinos
dungarees
flares
jeans
leggings
skinny jeans

And...
bow tie
braces
dressing gown
gloves
kimono
knickers
nightshirt
pants
pyjamas
scarf
shorts
tie

sleeve
buckle
socks
zip
pleat
strap
cuff
pocket
shoelaces

Writing about clothes

dirty *(adjective)*
My clothes are <u>dirty</u> because I've been gardening.

grubby
mucky
muddy

fashion *(noun)*
They followed the latest <u>fashion</u>.

look
style
trend

fashionable *(adjective)*
You always wear such <u>fashionable</u> outfits.

stylish
trendy

loose *(adjective)*
She likes to wear <u>loose</u> shirts.

baggy
roomy

neat *(adjective)*
You look very <u>neat</u> in your suit.

smart
groomed
tidy

scruffy *(adjective)*
That old dress is very <u>scruffy</u>.

messy
shabby
tatty
ragged
tattered

stain *(noun)*
There was a grease <u>stain</u> on his shirt.

mark
spot

tight *(adjective)*
Are my skinny jeans too <u>tight</u>?

clingy
fitted
snug
tight-fitting

Clothes can also be...
casual
elegant
formal
frilly

Getting dressed words

bare *(adjective)*
The baby was <u>bare</u> except for his nappy.

naked
nude
undressed

take off *(verb)*
He had to <u>take off</u> his wet jeans.

remove

tie *(verb)*
The girl struggled to <u>tie</u> her shoes.

do up
fasten
lace

undo *(verb)*
I can't <u>undo</u> my trousers.

loosen
open
unbutton
untie
unzip

wear *(verb)*
What clothes are you going to <u>wear</u>?

put on

fabric *(noun)*
The shirt was made from an unusual <u>fabric</u>.

cloth
material

Types of fabric...
chintz
corduroy
cotton
lace
linen
satin
silk
taffeta
velour
velvet

pattern *(noun)*
I like the bird <u>pattern</u> on your T-shirt.

design
decoration
motif

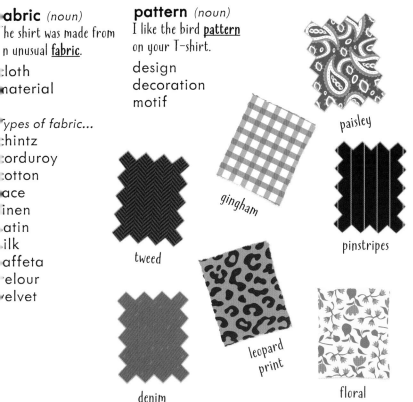

paisley

gingham

tweed

pinstripes

leopard print

denim

floral

polka dots

Food words

ripe cherries

plump apricots

food *(noun)*
grub
nourishment

drink *(noun)*
What <u>drink</u> would
you like?
beverage
refreshment

drink *(verb)*
Please <u>drink</u> the rest
of the juice.
gulp
guzzle
sip

eat *(verb)*
Don't <u>eat</u> that!
bite
chew
chomp
devour
gobble
munch
nibble
scoff
swallow

fruit *(noun)*
Types of fruit:
apple
apricot
avocado
banana
blackberry
blackcurrant
blueberry
cherry
clementine
date
fig
gooseberry

grapes
grapefruit
greengage
kiwi fruit
lemon
lime
lychee
mandarin
mango
melon
nectarine
orange
papaya

peach
pear
pineapple
plum
pomegranate
raspberry
rhubarb
satsuma
star fruit
strawberry
tomato

juicy watermelon

meal *(noun)*
That <u>meal</u>
was delicious.
banquet
barbecue
buffet
feast
picnic

dessert *(noun)*
What's for <u>dessert</u>?
pudding
sweet

meat *(noun)*
Types of meat:
bacon
beef
burger
chicken
chop

duck
gammon
goose
ham
lamb
mince
mutton

pheasant
pork
sausage
steak
turkey
venison

spicy sausages

crisp lettuce

vegetable

(noun)

greens

Types of vegetable:

artichoke
asparagus
aubergine
beetroot
broad beans
broccoli
cabbage

carrot
cauliflower
celery
courgette
garlic
leek
lettuce
mangetout
mushroom
onion
parsnip
peas

pepper
potato
pumpkin
radish
spinach
spring onion
squash
sweet corn
turnip

Types of spices:

cardamom
cinnamon
cloves
cumin

chilli
nutmeg
paprika
saffron
turmeric

Types of herbs:

basil
bay leaves
coriander

parsley
rosemary
sage
thyme

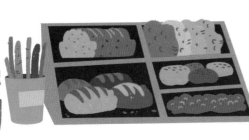

freshly caught fish

bread *(noun)*

Types of bread:

baguette
bread stick
cob
loaf

naan
pitta
roll
tortilla

crusty bread

fish *(noun)*

Types of fish:

cod
haddock
hake
halibut
herring
mackerel

pilchard
plaice
pollock
salmon
sardine
sea bass
trout
tuna

shellfish

Describing food

YUM

eww

PFFFF

bitter (adjective)
The **bitter** drink made my lips pucker.

sharp
sour
tart

disgusting
(adjective)
Yuck. This hot dog is **disgusting**.

foul
revolting
vile

full of (adjective)
The loaf is **full of** raisins.

filled with
stuffed with
packed with
crammed with

greasy (adjective)
The stew is rather **greasy**.

fatty
oily

hot (adjective)
Eat carefully! The pizza is **hot**.

piping hot
sizzling

mild (adjective)
I can't taste the garlic. It's too **mild**.

bland
delicate
faint
subtle

raw (adjective)
The beef is **raw**.

bloody
underdone
uncooked

spicy (adjective)
Did you find the pie too **spicy**?

hot
peppery

stale (adjective)
The man said the bread was **stale**.

mouldy
past its best

sweet (adjective)
The pastry in the tart is too **sweet**.

sugary
cloying

taste (noun)
This cheese has a strange **taste**.

flavour
tang

taste (verb)
Could you **taste** the sauce?

sample
sip
test
try

tasty (adjective)
I've never had such a **tasty** trifle.

delicious
appetizing
mouthwatering
scrumptious
yummy

thick (adjective)
The custard is **thick**.

lumpy
congealed
stodgy

thin (adjective)
The soup is **thin**.

runny
watery

Food can also be...
buttery
chewy
creamy
crisp
crumbly
crunchy
flavourless
fluffy
gooey
juicy
leathery
mushy
nourishing
plain
rich
salty
seasoned
sloppy
spongy
squidgy
sticky
succulent
sweet-and-sour
tender
tough
vinegary
zesty
zingy

Cooking

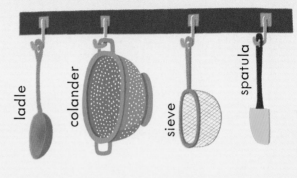

ladle colander sieve spatula

amount *(noun)*
What <u>amount</u> of butter is required?
quantity

blob *(noun)*
Add a <u>blob</u> of batter to the pan.
lump
dollop
splodge

cook *(verb)*
Who wants to <u>cook</u> lunch?
make
prepare
put together

cool *(verb)*
<u>Cool</u> the melted butter before adding.
chill
refrigerate

difficult *(adjective)*
The recipe for puff pastry is <u>difficult</u>.
hard
complicated
complex
tricky

easy *(adjective)*
It's an <u>easy</u> recipe.
simple
straightforward
uncomplicated

extra *(adjective)*
I think that it needs <u>extra</u> seasoning.
more
further
additional

fill *(verb)*
Can you <u>fill</u> the jug with milk?
refill
replenish
top up

heat *(verb)*
<u>Heat</u> the milk gently in a pan.
warm up

instructions *(noun)*
Follow the <u>instructions</u> in the recipe.
directions

main *(adjective)*
The <u>main</u> ingredient is rice.
chief
key
major

mash *(verb)*
<u>Mash</u> the potatoes with a fork.
crush
pound
pulp

organize *(verb)*
Who will <u>organize</u> the dinner?
arrange
plan
prepare
set up

pour *(verb)*
<u>Pour</u> the water into the flour.
add
tip

serve *(verb)*
Would you <u>serve</u> the carrots, please?
dish up
pass round

stir *(verb)*
<u>Stir</u> the eggs together first.
beat
whip
whisk

When people cook, they may...
bake
barbecue
boil
fry
grill
poach
roast
scramble
steam
stir-fry

He stirred the sauce methodically.

chef's hat

chef's whites/ uniform

cup *(noun)*
Types of cup:
beaker
glass
goblet
mug
tumbler

box *(noun)*
carton
container
packet

Fun and hobbies

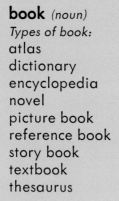
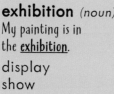

book (noun)
Types of book:
atlas
dictionary
encyclopedia
novel
picture book
reference book
story book
textbook
thesaurus

club (noun)
The drama <u>club</u> has over fifty members.
group
society

computer (noun)
Types of computer:
laptop
PC
tablet

diary (noun)
Do you like to keep a <u>diary</u>?
journal
record

draw (verb)
I want to <u>draw</u> another picture.
sketch
doodle

exhibition (noun)
My painting is in the <u>exhibition</u>.
display
show

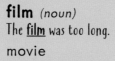

film (noun)
The <u>film</u> was too long.
movie

Types of films:
action film
adventure film
cartoon
comedy
horror film
romance
sci-fi
thriller
Western

fun (noun)
What do you do for <u>fun</u>?
entertainment
pleasure
recreation

hobby (noun)
Cooking is my <u>hobby</u> of choice.
activity
interest
pastime

Some hobbies:
bird watching
cooking
dancing
drama
fishing
football
gardening
knitting
origami
painting
photography
reading
sewing

party (noun)
Did you enjoy the <u>party</u>?
celebration
gathering
reception

photo (noun)
The best <u>photo</u> won a prize.
photograph
picture
snapshot

picture (noun)
That's a good <u>picture</u>.
drawing
painting
landscape
portrait
cartoon
sketch

relax (verb)
Knitting helps me to <u>relax</u>.
take it easy
unwind

story (noun)
It's soothing to read a <u>story</u> before bed.
tale

Types of story:
adventure story
detective story
fairy tale
fantasy story
ghost story
mystery

Job words

job *(noun)*
career
occupation
profession

 doctor

 pilot

 artist

 vet

 builder

 architect

scientist

hairdresser

 waiter

 firefighter

 mechanic

 gardener

 dentist

 nurse

 photographer

 farmer

 chef

 receptionist

Other jobs:
accountant
beautician
butcher
carpenter
designer
electrician

engineer
estate agent
journalist
lawyer
librarian
musician
pharmacist

plumber
police officer
secretary
shopkeeper
social worker
teacher
zookeeper

boss *(noun)*
His **boss** said the man was always late.
director
manager
supervisor

inspect *(verb)*
An official came to **inspect** their work.
check
examine
investigate
monitor
survey
study

unemployed
(adjective)
She had been **unemployed** for a month.
out of a job
out of work

work *(noun)*
Building is hard **work**.
labour
toil

work *(verb)*
My sisters **work** in a bank.
have a job
earn a living
go to work

Sport words

sport *(noun)*
exercise

Types of sport:
archery
athletics
badminton
baseball
basketball
boxing
cricket
cycling
diving
football
golf
gymnastics
hockey
ice hockey
judo
karate
netball
rowing
rugby
skating
skiing
snooker
squash
swimming
table tennis
tennis
volleyball

Sports venues:
arena
court
field
ice rink
pitch
ring
stadium
swimming pool
track

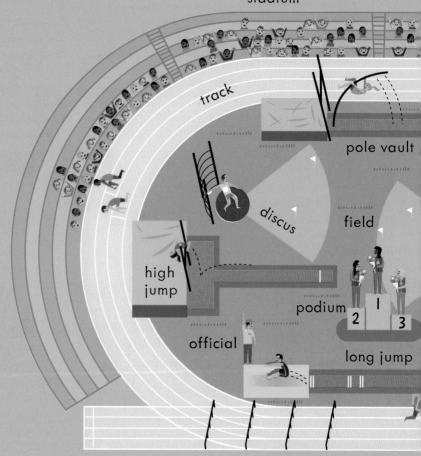

stadium
track
pole vault
discus
field
high jump
podium
official
long jump
hurdles

Describing athletes

athlete *(noun)*
Which <u>athlete</u> will win?

competitor
contestant
participant
player
runner
sportsman
sportswoman
swimmer

best *(adjective)*
The <u>best</u> runner won the race.

finest
top

skill *(noun)*
The high jumper showed such <u>skill</u>.

ability
talent

sporty *(adjective)*
She had always been very <u>sporty</u>.

athletic
energetic
fit

winner *(noun)*
The <u>winner</u> took the trophy.

champion
victor

medals

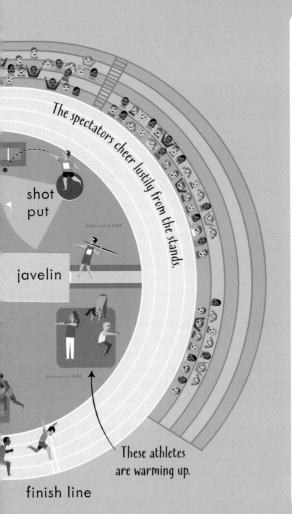

The spectators cheer lustily from the stands.

shot put

javelin

These athletes are warming up.

finish line

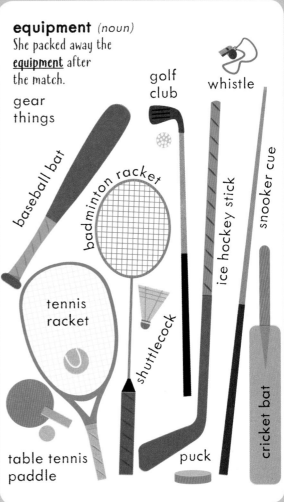

equipment *(noun)*
She packed away the <u>equipment</u> after the match.

gear
things

baseball bat

badminton racket

golf club

whistle

ice hockey stick

snooker cue

tennis racket

shuttlecock

cricket bat

table tennis paddle

puck

Things athletes do

beat *(verb)*
I will <u>beat</u> the others.

defeat
thrash

cheat *(verb)*
Please don't <u>cheat</u>.

break the rules

dive *(verb)*
He tried to <u>dive</u> for the ball.

lunge

hit *(verb)*
Try to <u>hit</u> the ball with your racket.

knock
strike
tap
touch

kick *(verb)*
Can you <u>kick</u> the ball?

dribble
pass

lift *(verb)*
Let's <u>lift</u> him up so he can catch the ball.

hoist
raise

lose *(verb)*
They will <u>lose</u> again.

be beaten
be defeated
suffer defeat

play *(verb)*
The team will <u>play</u> their rivals.

challenge
play against
take on

trophy/cup

75

At the circus

amuse *(verb)*
The strongmen __amuse__ the crowds.

delight
entertain

face *(noun)*
Look at the acrobat's concentrated __face__.

expression

joke *(noun)*
Her __joke__ was funnier than his.

gag
pun

laugh *(verb)*
The show made us __laugh__.

chuckle
giggle
chortle
snigger
titter

tease *(verb)*
The clowns __tease__ each other.

laugh at
make fun of

trick *(noun)*
His __trick__ was astonishing.

stunt

Circus acts...
do magic tricks
perform
take a bow

Circus acts perform for the crowds inside the big top.

Daring trapeze artists swing through the air.

An acrobat gingerly steps along the tightrope.

The ringmaster announces the acts.

The audience gasps.

ahhhhh

OOOOOOO

Next in the ring...

juggler

The strongman flexes his bulging muscles.

unicycle

76

Dance words

dance *(verb)*
Shall we <u>dance</u>?
- boogie
- bop
- jig about
- move to the music

Line dancers move in time together.

Ballet dancers are graceful and light on their feet.

tutu

ballet tights

leotard

leg warmers

A street dancer balances on one hand.

The flamenco dancer's frilly dress swishes from side to side.

People who dance together are each other's partners.

dance cane

top hat

tap shoes

spin *(verb)*
The dancer could <u>spin</u> on one foot.
- go round
- turn
- twirl
- twist
- pirouette

Dancers may...
- glide
- gyrate
- jiggle
- prance
- shuffle
- stomp
- swing
- wiggle

Dancers can be...
- agile
- balletic
- elegant
- graceful
- lithe
- nimble
- sprightly

Music

group (noun)
What's your favourite <u>group</u>?

act
band
choir
orchestra

musician (noun)
Each <u>musician</u> in the band played a different instrument.

performer
player

Types of musician:
cellist
drummer
fiddler
flautist
guitarist
organist
pianist
soloist
trumpeter
violinist

Things musicians do

fade (verb)
The sound of the choir began to <u>fade</u>.

diminish
disappear
dwindle
grow faint
wane

perform (verb)
The orchestra will <u>perform</u> after the interval.

play
appear

practise (verb)
The violinist had to <u>practise</u> her solo.

rehearse
go over
prepare
fine tune

Song words

sing (verb)
Her mother would always <u>sing</u> at parties.

serenade
warble

singer (noun)
Who is the lead <u>singer</u>?

vocalist

Types of singer:
alto
baritone
bass
soprano
tenor
treble

song (noun)
What <u>song</u> are you singing?

ditty
melody
tune

Describing music and musicians

Styles of music:
country
folk
hip hop
jazz
musical
opera
pop
rap
reggae
rhythm and blues
rock

clear (adjective)
The tenor has such a <u>clear</u> voice.

distinct
audible
recognizable

famous (adjective)
Have you heard of that <u>famous</u> pianist?

celebrated
renowned
well-known
world-famous

Music can be...
catchy
classical
dramatic
enchanting
haunting
improvised
joyful
repetitive
rousing
rhythmic
shrill
tuneful

The guitarist uses a plectrum to pluck the strings on his guitar.

microphone

WOW!

amplifier

Musical instruments

A large group of musicians play together in an orchestra.

grand piano

chime

tuba

trumpet

trombone

harp

bass drum

flute

clarinet

baton

double bass

bow

cello

violins

A conductor helps an orchestra play together.

String instruments	Brass instruments	Wind instruments	Percussion instruments	Keyboard instruments
cello	bugle	bagpipes	bass drum	accordion
double bass	cornet	bassoon	chimes	electric organ
guitar	euphonium	clarinet	cymbals	harpsichord
harp	french horn	flute	glockenspiel	piano
sitar	trombone	harmonica	kettle drum	organ
ukulele	trumpet	oboe	triangle	synthesizer
viola	tuba	recorder	wood block	
violin		saxophone	xylophone	

Science lab

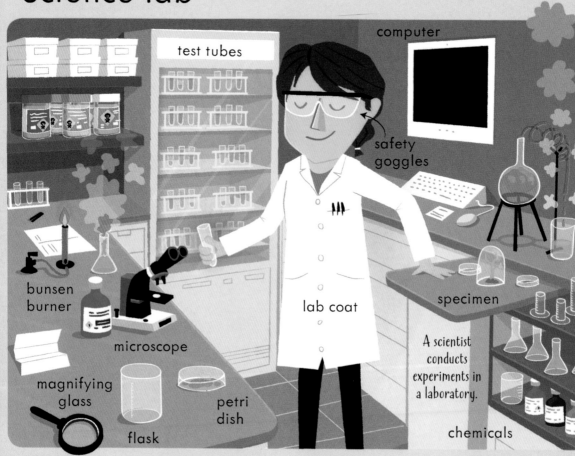

computer

test tubes

safety goggles

bunsen burner

microscope

lab coat

specimen

magnifying glass

petri dish

A scientist conducts experiments in a laboratory.

flask

chemicals

drip *(verb)*
Liquid began to **drip**.

dribble
leak
ooze
trickle

effect *(noun)*
What **effect** will heat have on the metal?

consequence
result

happen *(verb)*
What will **happen** if you add water?

come about
occur
take place

invent *(verb)*
The professor will **invent** a new machine.

create
design
devise

machine *(noun)*
The **machine** made a whirring sound.

appliance
gadget
contraption

mix *(verb)*
You must **mix** the two chemicals together.

blend
combine

poisonous
(adjective)
The gas is **poisonous**.

deadly
harmful
toxic

prove *(verb)*
Can you **prove** which material is strongest?

confirm
demonstrate
show

runny *(adjective)*
The mixture is **runny**.

liquid
molten
sloppy

sure *(adjective)*
I'm **sure** it'll work.

certain
confident
convinced
hopeful

think about *(verb)*
They had to **think about** the experiment's results.

consider
contemplate
ponder

tool *(noun)*
Which **tool** do you want?

implement
instrument
utensil

Robots

oud *(adjective)*
he **loud** robot could be
eard from far away.

noisy
booming

shake *(verb)*
The robot started to **shake**
as it came to life.

rattle
shudder
vibrate

switch *(noun)*
Use the **switch** to turn
the robot on.

button
control
knob

turn *(verb)*
Four cogs **turn** inside
the robot's head.

go round
rotate

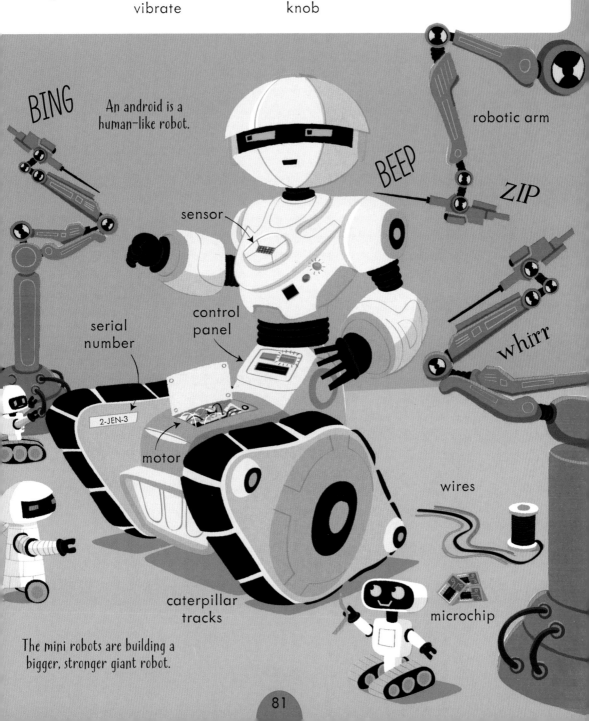

BING

An android is a
human-like robot.

robotic arm

BEEP

ZIP

sensor

whirr

control
panel

serial
number

motor

wires

caterpillar
tracks

microchip

2-JEN-3

The mini robots are building a
bigger, stronger giant robot.

Spooky words

spooky *(adjective)*
This place is too **spooky** for me.

creepy
eerie
frightening
scary
terrifying

A vampire bat winged its way across the dark night sky.

full moon

HOOOOWWWL

cobweb

lantern

werewolf

coffin

R.I.P.

tombstone

skeleton hand

vampire

pumpkin

Spooky places

creak *(verb)*
The hinges **creak** as I open the door.

groan
squeak

dim *(adjective)*
The graveyard was dark and **dim**.

dingy
gloomy
shadowy

old *(adjective)*
The **old** house stood alone on a hill.

ancient
crumbling
dilapidated

strange *(adjective)*
A **strange** noise came from inside the coffin.

mysterious
odd
peculiar
unusual

WHOOO

bat

haunted house

AAAAAAHHH

boil

POP

bubble

raven

zombie

cauldron

black cat

toad

Writing about spooky things

awful *(adjective)*
He'd never seen such an **awful** sight.
dreadful
gruesome
horrid
revolting
terrible

evil *(adjective)*
The **evil** witch sneered.
cruel
vile
wicked

ghost *(noun)*
The **ghost** flew out from the shadows.
ghoul
phantom
spirit

scare *(verb)*
"You can't **scare** me," yelled Amelia.
frighten
petrify
spook
startle
terrify

scream *(verb)*
Someone suddenly started to **scream**.
howl
shriek
screech
wail

shake *(verb)*
She began to **shake** with fear.
tremble
shudder
quake

Vampires...
have fangs
suck blood
wear capes

Witches...
cackle
cast spells
have warty skin
ride broomsticks

Ghosts...
float
haunt
vanish

Fairytale words

toadstool house

fairy

Fairies flit and flutter, and sprinkle fairy dust.

elf

pixie

adventure *(noun)*
The hero described his last **adventure**.

exploit
feat
quest

anger *(noun)*
The giant bared his teeth in **anger**.

fury
indignation
rage
wrath

astonish *(verb)*
The riches inside the palace will **astonish** you.

amaze
astound
dazzle
stun

beware of *(verb)*
Beware of the three-headed dog.

look out for
steer clear of
watch out for

charm *(verb)*
The fairy queen cast a spell to **charm** the goblins.

beguile
bewitch
enchant
mesmerize

grand *(adjective)*
We spied a **grand** castle through the trees.

fabulous
impressive
magnificent
splendid

hold *(verb)*
She couldn't **hold** her wand for fear.

clasp
clutch
grasp
grip

imaginary *(adjective)*
All kinds of **imaginary** creatures live here.

fantastic
make-believe
fictional
mythical

magic *(noun)*
The wizard had studied **magic** all his life.

sorcery
witchcraft
wizardry

real *(adjective)*
The events in this story are not all **real**.

factual
genuine
true
truthful

spell *(noun)*
She muttered a **spell** under her breath.

charm
curse
magic formula

vanish *(verb)*
How did the pixie **vanish**?

disappear
vanish into thin air
become invisible

Fairytale places

castle
cave
dell
dungeon
magical forest
maze
palace
secret passage
tower
treasure room
tunnel
under the sea

Story starters

"Who will rescue my son?"
sobbed the queen...

King Rex hadn't left his
castle for ten years...

enchanted
palace

Long, long ago in
a magical land...

Characters and creatures

witch *(noun)*
The wicked <u>witch</u>
cast an evil spell.

crone
sorceress

wizard *(noun)*
The <u>wizard</u> stroked
his beard.

magician
sorcerer

Other characters:
dragon
dwarf
elf
giant
goblin
king
knight
magician
mermaid
ogre
prince
princess
queen
troll
unicorn

*Fairytale characters
can be...*
bewitching
creepy
cunning
evil
invisible
kindly
legendary
magical
menacing
under a spell
wicked
wise

*Fairytale characters
can...*
come to the
 rescue
do battle
have dreams
outwit each other
rescue captives
solve riddles
grant wishes
turn people into
 stone

Magical things

cloak
crystal ball
lucky charm
magic potions
magic ring
pointed hat
spell book
staff
wand

snort

The dragon slept on the gleaming
treasure with one eye always open.

Dinosaurs

Pterosaurs could fly.

Brachiosaurus

Diplodocus

Tyrannosaurus rex

Triceratops

claw

Velociraptor

dinosaur eggs

Dinosaurs lived on land.

Stegosaurus

Describing dinosaurs

fierce *(adjective)*
A fierce Tyrannosaurus loomed above.

aggressive
ferocious
savage
vicious

huge *(adjective)*
Brachiosaurus had a **huge** body.

colossal
enormous
gigantic
massive

strong *(adjective)*
The dinosaur snapped with its **strong** jaws.

mighty
powerful

Dinosaurs can also be...
feathery
meat-eating
scaly

Things dinosaurs do

attack *(verb)*
Velociraptors **attack** each other.

charge at
set upon

land on *(verb)*
The pterosaurs **land on** high branches.

fly down onto
settle on

scratch *(verb)*
They **scratch** the dust with their claws.

gouge
mark
scrape

stare *(verb)*
They **stare** at their prey.

gape
gaze

Jurassic squid

Plesiosaurs lived in the sea.

Cavemen

cave (noun)
cavern

Inside the cave it's safe and warm, while outside wild animals roam.

stalactite

volcano

cave painting

explode (verb)
Lava began to **explode** from the crater.

erupt
spew

woolly mammoth

sabre-toothed tiger

pick (verb)
Some cavemen **pick** wild berries.

collect
forage
gather
pluck

wild (adjective)
They hide from a **wild** cat.

feral
untamed

stop (verb)
They **stop** hunting and go back home.

finish
give up
quit

stalagmite

burn (verb)
The logs in the fire **burn** bright.

blaze
glow
smoulder

animal skin

shelter (noun)
They find **shelter** in the cave.

cover
protection
refuge

spear

Ancient Egypt

age *(noun)*
The pyramid was built in the Ancient Egyptian <u>age</u>.

era
period
time

discover *(verb)*
When did they <u>discover</u> the tomb?

find
locate
uncover
unearth

fragile *(adjective)*
The jar was made from <u>fragile</u> clay.

breakable
brittle
delicate

important *(adjective)*
An <u>important</u> nobleman was buried here.

distinguished
notable
remarkable
significant
special

rich *(adjective)*
<u>Rich</u> Egyptians had lots of servants.

affluent
wealthy
well-off

tunnel *(noun)*
A long <u>tunnel</u> led to the chamber.

passage
passageway
shaft

Deep inside a pyramid lay a pharaoh's tomb.

gold coffin

The mummy stirred to life.

statue of Anubis (an Egyptian god)

chest

sarcophagus (a large stone coffin)

hieroglyphs

scarab beetles

Vikings

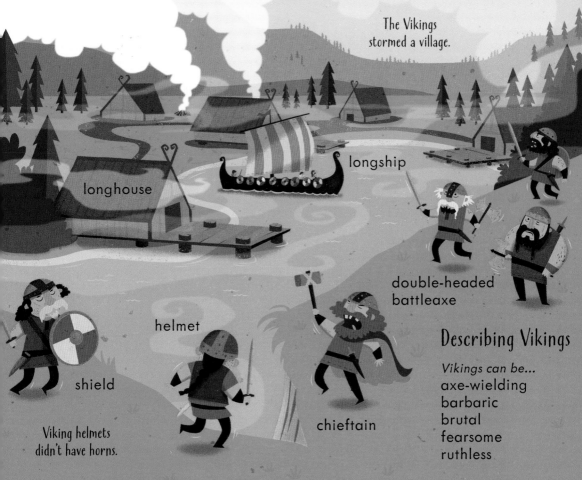

The Vikings stormed a village.

longship

longhouse

double-headed battleaxe

helmet

shield

Viking helmets didn't have horns.

chieftain

Describing Vikings

Vikings can be...
axe-wielding
barbaric
brutal
fearsome
ruthless

argue *(verb)*
"Don't <u>argue</u>!" ordered the chief.

bicker
quarrel
row
squabble

crowd *(noun)*
A <u>crowd</u> of Vikings set sail.

gang
group
horde
throng

danger *(noun)*
They overcame one <u>danger</u> after another.

hazard
peril
threat
trouble

free *(verb)*
<u>Free</u> the captives!

liberate
release
set free

invade *(verb)*
They're about to <u>invade</u> the town.

attack
overrun
plunder
raid
storm
take over

store *(noun)*
They ransacked the town's <u>store</u> of grain.

hoard
stock
supply

Viking names

Female names:
Astrid
Dagrun
Gudrun
Hilde
Saga
Sigrid

Male names:
Gunnar
Harald
Knut
Leif
Olav
Ulf

Wild West

The sheriff stepped out through the swinging doors.

The cowgirls fled on horseback.

covered wagon

Howdy

arrest *(verb)*
The sheriff and his deputy plotted to <u>arrest</u> the gang.

catch
capture
apprehend

cunning *(adjective)*
The <u>cunning</u> cowboy sneaked by unnoticed.

crafty
devious
sly
sneaky
wily

escape *(verb)*
How did they <u>escape</u>?

break free
flee
get away
run away

fight *(noun)*
Everyone stopped to watch the <u>fight</u>.

brawl
scuffle
tussle

gang *(noun)*
A <u>gang</u> of cowgirls rode into town.

club
group
mob
posse

jail *(noun)*
The man went to <u>jail</u> for rustling cattle.

a lock up
prison

luck *(noun)*
The cowboy hit the target by <u>luck</u>.

accident
chance
coincidence
fluke

meeting *(noun)*
The deputy summoned everyone to a <u>meeting</u>.

assembly
gathering

robber *(noun)*
The <u>robber</u> was behind bars at last.

thief
burglar
criminal
crook
bandit

shock *(noun)*
It was a <u>shock</u> when he won the rodeo.

surprise
bombshell

steal *(verb)*
The thief tried to <u>steal</u> the gold.

grab
snatch
seize
make off with

surprise *(verb)*
Did her horse's speed <u>surprise</u> you?

shock
stun
startle

lasso

cowboy boots

WANTED

REWARD
$1,000

wanted poster

YEE HAW

sheriff's badge

handlebar moustache

Characters
cattle rustler
   (someone who
   steals cows)
cowboys
cowgirls
sheriff
deputy
townspeople

spurs

bull riding

Story endings

Clutching his wounded arm,
the lone cowboy stumbled
into the sunset.

The outlaws mounted
their horses and rode
away in a cloud of dust.

The town of
Little Cactus would never
be the same again.

Ancient Greeks

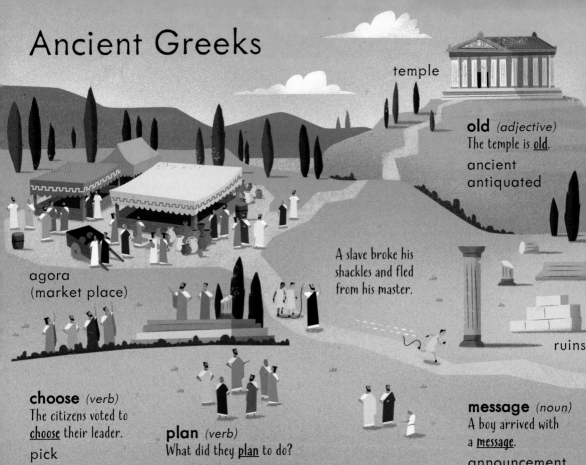

temple

old *(adjective)*
The temple is <u>old</u>.

ancient
antiquated

agora
(market place)

A slave broke his
shackles and fled
from his master.

ruins

choose *(verb)*
The citizens voted to
<u>choose</u> their leader.

pick
elect
appoint
select

plan *(verb)*
What did they <u>plan</u> to do?

intend
mean
resolve

message *(noun)*
A boy arrived with
a <u>message</u>.

announcement
letter
note
report

Zeus (king of
the gods)

Ancient Greek religion

god *(noun)*
The Ancient Greeks
believed in more
than one <u>god</u>.

deity
divinity

religion *(noun)*
Their <u>religion</u> has
lots of stories.

belief
faith

Some Greek gods:
Aphrodite (goddess of love)
Apollo (god of music)
Ares (god of war)
Athena (goddess of wisdom)
Hades (god of the underworld)
Hera (queen of the gods)
Poseidon (god of the sea)

Artemis
(goddess of
hunting)

Hermes
(messenger o
the gods)

Romans

denarius
(a silver coin)

A Roman man wore a long
length of cloth, or toga.

laurel
wreath

emperor
(ruler of Roman
empire)

toga

scroll

senator
(politician)

A Roman woman wore a long
dress called a stola.

Roman names

Augusta
Claudius
Commodus
Faustina
Flavia
Lesbia
Marcus
Octavius
Pompeia
Publius

Male names end in -us and
female names in -a.

fight *(verb)*
They watched the
gladiators <u>fight</u>.
brawl
scuffle
tussle
wrestle

forgive *(verb)*
Will the emperor <u>forgive</u>
the gladiator if he loses?
excuse
let off
pardon

powerful
(adjective)
He was a <u>powerful</u> ruler.
commanding
forceful
mighty

rebel *(verb)*
The emperor feared the
people would <u>rebel</u>.
revolt
riot
rise up

gladius
(a sword)

shield

trident (three-
pronged spear)

net

Gladiators fought
in an arena at an
amphitheatre.

spear

chariot

93

In space

astronaut *(noun)*
The <u>astronaut</u> put on his helmet.

spaceman
cosmonaut

explore *(verb)*
Their mission was to <u>explore</u> outer space.

search
tour

go round *(verb)*
Moons <u>go round</u> planets.

orbit
travel around

shine *(verb)*
Stars <u>shine</u> brightly in the sky.

gleam
glimmer
glow
sparkle
twinkle

spaceship *(noun)*
The <u>spaceship</u> landed on the moon.

rocket
spacecraft

Spaceships may...
take off
blast off
touch down
zoom

Planets can be...
airless
fiery
frozen
icy
rocky

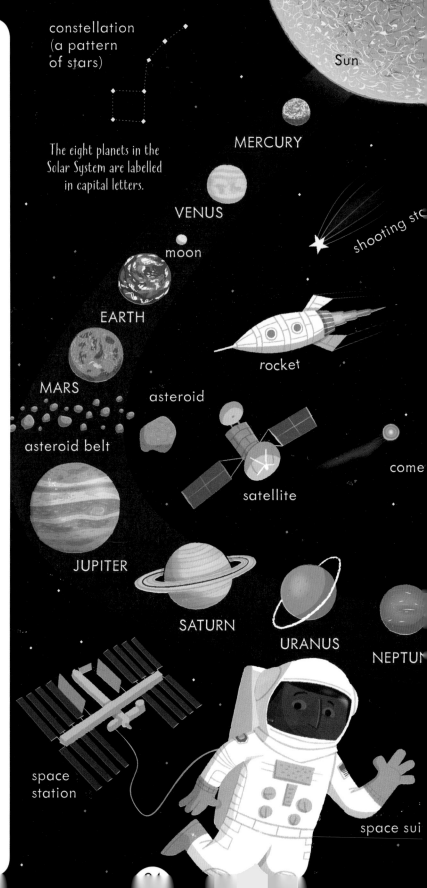

constellation (a pattern of stars)

The eight planets in the Solar System are labelled in capital letters.

Sun

MERCURY

VENUS

moon

shooting sto

EARTH

rocket

MARS

asteroid

asteroid belt

satellite

come

JUPITER

SATURN

URANUS

NEPTUN

space station

space sui

Aliens

flying saucer

alien *(noun)*
martian
space creature
extraterrestrial
lifeform

The laser beam was
dead on target.

TAKE THAT

ZAP

bleep

bleep

laser gun

antenna

UFO
(Unidentified
Flying Object)

WHOOOSH

ray gun

controls

Toxic gas
billowed from
the crater.

Describing aliens

evil *(adjective)*
The **evil** aliens
plotted revenge.

nasty
fiendish
wicked

friendly *(adjective)*
The **friendly** alien
came in peace.

gentle
good-natured
kind

Aliens can also be...
green-skinned
one-eyed
slimy
spotty
superintelligent

Things aliens and flying saucers do

attack *(verb)*
hostile creatures
attack the planet.

invade
bombard
storm

bang *(noun)*
His spacecraft landed
with a **bang**.

crash
thud
thump

flash *(verb)*
Flames **flash** from
the engine.

blaze
burst
flare

shoot *(verb)*
Some flying saucers
shoot lasers.

aim
direct
fire

Pirates

Pirates are...

adventurous
barbaric
bloodthirsty
bold
brutal
daring
dastardly
lawless
ruthless
swashbuckling
villainous

Pirates...
board ships
bury treasure
drop anchor
make prisoners
 walk the plank
plunder
raid
swab (clean) the
 deck
take prisoners

Pirate ships

crew (noun)
The crew set sail
for home.
sailors
seafarers
mariners

flap (verb)
Sails flap in the wind.
flutter
ripple
swish

sail (verb)
The ship began to sail.
cruise
glide
ride the waves

sink (verb)
I fear the ship will sink.
capsize
go under
founder
submerge

Sea words

crash (verb)
Can you hear the
waves crash?
roar
rumble
thunder

sea (noun)
They sailed across
the sea.
high seas
main
ocean
waves

sharp (adjective)
Sharp rocks ahead!
craggy
jagged

splash (verb)
The waves splash on
the shore.
slap
spill

wave (noun)
The bottle was carried
by the wave.
breaker
surf
swell

wavy (adjective)
The sea is wavy today.
choppy
fierce
rough
wild

Treasure words

chest (noun)
The treasure chest was
full to the brim.
case
casket
coffer
trunk

shiny (adjective)
The shiny treasure
glinted in the sun.
dazzling
gleaming
glittering
shining
polished
shimmering
sparkling

treasure (noun)
Captain Patch dreamed
of treasure.
bounty
loot
riches

Items of treasure:
coins
ducats
doubloons
goblets
gold
jewels
medallions
pieces of eight
silver

Story starters

"Gold beyond your wildest dreams!"
promised the captain...

The treasure map was
theirs at last...

Two ships were racing
towards Porpoise Island...

97

Heroes and villains

MEET THE HEROES...

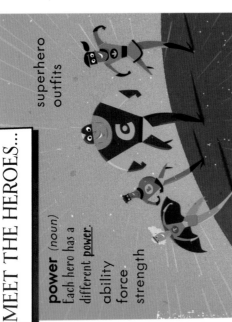

superhero outfits

power *(noun)*
Each hero has a different <u>power</u>.

ability
force
strength

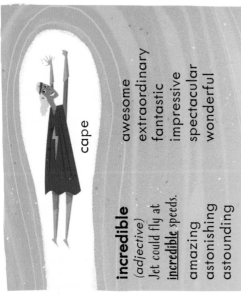

cape

incredible *(adjective)*
Jet could fly at <u>incredible</u> speeds.

amazing
astonishing
astounding

awesome
extraordinary
fantastic
impressive
spectacular
wonderful

nimble *(adjective)*
Basilisk is <u>nimble</u> on his feet.

acrobatic
agile
light-footed

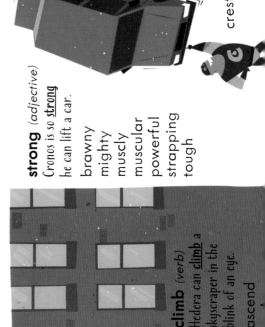

crest

strong *(adjective)*
Cronos is so <u>strong</u> he can lift a car.

brawny
mighty
muscly
muscular
powerful
strapping
tough

climb *(verb)*
Hedera can <u>climb</u> a skyscraper in the blink of an eye.

ascend

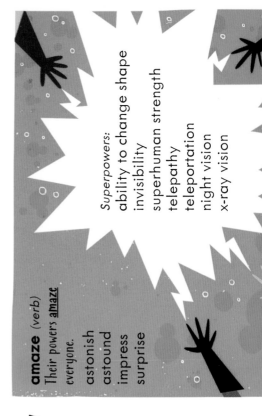

amaze *(verb)*
Their powers <u>amaze</u> everyone.

astonish
astound
impress
surprise

Superpowers:
ability to change shape
invisibility
superhuman strength
telepathy
teleportation
night vision
x-ray vision

villain *(adjective)*
A villain plots in his lair.

baddie
criminal
mastermind
crook
mischief-maker
scoundrel

proud *(adjective)*
He's as proud as he's cunning.

arrogant
haughty
pompous
smug
vain

boast *(verb)*
He dares to boast about his plan.

brag
gloat

help *(verb)*
"Who will help us?" the people cry out.

aid
assist
support

disaster *(noun)*
Disaster threatens the city.

calamity
catastrophe
tragedy

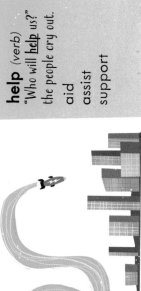

defend *(verb)*
"We will defend you!"

protect
shield

punch *(verb)*
Together they punch the missile and knock it off course.

hit
jab
smack
strike
thump
thwack

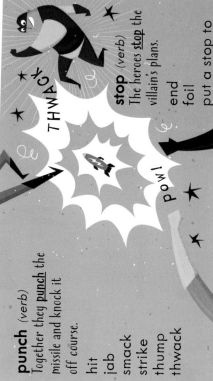

THWACK

POW!

stop *(verb)*
The heroes stop the villain's plans.

end
foil
put a stop to

THE END

save *(verb)*
When will the heroes have to save the city again?

rescue

Knights and castles

Describing knights

alert (adjective)
Sir Gawain was ready and **alert**.

attentive
watchful
wide-awake

brave (adjective)
There was no knight more **brave**.

bold
courageous
daring
gallant
heroic
plucky

cruel (adjective)
The **cruel** knight vowed revenge on the whole town.

callous
merciless
pitiless
ruthless

Knights can also be...
chivalrous
fearless
honourable
lionhearted
noble
quick-witted

Armour and weapons

flail
mace
plume
helmet
breastplate
chainmail
gauntlet
shield
greave
dagger
broadsword
spur

Things knights do

courage (noun)
Knights show great **courage**.

bravery
fearlessness
valour

fight (verb)
Armies of knights will **fight**.

clash
cross swords
do battle
take up arms
wage war

guard (verb)
He was told to **guard** the gate.

defend
protect
watch

mission (noun)
The knights were training for their next **mission**.

adventure
expedition
quest

stab (verb)
A knight can **stab** his sword.

jab
lunge with
thrust

swear (verb)
Will you **swear** to protect the king?

promise
vow

In battle

enemy (noun)
The army fought the **enemy** for days.

opponent
opposition
other side

retreat (verb)
The soldiers began to **retreat**.

flee
move back
withdraw

At a joust

admire (verb)
The crowds **admire** the dashing knight.

look up to
marvel at
respect

cheer (verb)
They will **cheer** if he wins.

applaud
clap
whoop

turret

battlements

castle (*noun*)
chateau
fort
fortress
keep
palace
stronghold

moat

gatehouse

drawbridge

battle (*noun*)
clash
conflict
skirmish

battering ram

WHIZZ

A volley of arrows zip overhead.

catapult

archer

bow

standard (flag)

lord

lady

herald

lance

Two knights were competing in a joust.

Monsters

monster *(noun)*
beast
creature

Monsters can be...
bloodthirsty
deadly
fire-breathing
gigantic
hairy
long-necked
one-eyed
scaly
slimy
tough
wrinkly

Monsters can have...
claws
fangs
fur
hairy toes
horns
rotten breath
scales
spines
tails
warts
wings

A monster might live in a...
bog
castle
cave
dell
den
dungeon
forest
lair
lake
swamp
well
wood

dragon

flickering flames

troll

Monsters can be tiny too.

tentacle

bog monster

brutal *(adjective)*
Everyone feared the <u>brutal</u> creature.
brutish
fearsome
ferocious
fierce
savage

smell *(noun)*
A <u>smell</u> wafted from the ogre's boots.
odour
stench

stink *(verb)*
The goblin's clothes <u>stink</u>.
smell
reek
pong
whiff

tangled *(adjective)*
Its fur was greasy and <u>tangled</u>.
knotted
matted
twisted

tough *(adjective)*
That giant is a <u>tough</u> brute.
wild
rough
violent
vicious
hard

unpleasant *(adjective)*
The <u>unpleasant</u> troll lived by himself.
nasty
disagreeable
bad-tempered
spiteful

giant/ogre

monster
bug

club

goblin

gremlin

A cave monster lumbered
out from the shadows.

three-headed
serpent

Things monsters do

annoy *(verb)*
The gremlins **annoy**
the villagers.

pester
harass
harangue
trouble

lie *(verb)*
The deceitful goblin
couldn't but **lie**.

fib
tell lies
tell untruths

shock *(verb)*
Did its groans **shock**
you too?

alarm
scare
startle
surprise

smear *(verb)*
The swamp monsters
smear the walls
with gunk.

daub
rub
spread

squash *(verb)*
The giant tried to **squash**
the house with her foot.

crumple
crush
flatten
smash
squish
stamp on
trample on

temper *(noun)*
The grumpy monster is
in a bad **temper**.

mood
rage

Monsters can...
attack without
  warning
bellow
chomp on food
roar
scratch
slobber
snort
swish their tails

Writing tips

Write your own words

- You can join some words together to make new words.
- Add '-sounding', '-looking', '-smelling' or '-tasting' to the end of an adjective, to describe how something sounds, looks, smells or tastes.
- Add '-eating', '-hating', '-loving' or '-fearing' after a noun, to describe what something eats, hates, loves or fears.

shrill-sounding birds
a scrawny-looking cat
foul-smelling fruit
delicious-tasting doughnuts

a cheese-eating mouse
a postman-hating dog
slime-loving monsters
a clown-fearing ringmaster

BANG

POP

SCHLOOP SQUOP
(walking through a bog)

Sounds like

- Each of these words is an onomatopeia (say on-oh-mat-oh-pee-a).
- An onomatopeia when spoken sounds like the noise it describes.
- Spell out noises to make your own onomatopeia words.

KA-TWANG
(firing a catapult)

DIDDA-DUDDA-DIDDA-DUD
(typing)

Descriptive comparisons

- You can describe something by comparing it with something else. This is known as a simile.
  - Many similes start with 'like':

    Flames burst from the dragon's mouth like molten lava from an erupting volcano.

  - Similes can also start with 'as':

    The wet ground was as slippery as an ice rink.

Setting the scene

- Describe scenes as fully as you can when writing stories.

  Describe...
  - what the weather is like
  - what noises can be heard
  - how the surroundings look, smell, feel or taste

- You could turn to one of the scenes in this book and describe what you see, for instance on pages 82-83...

A bolt of lightning lit up the night sky revealing a lonely house on a hill. In the distance a wolf howled while bats squeaked overhead. The air around them was damp, and thick with the smell of rotten eggs...

Characters

- Describe your characters thoroughly to make them convincing.

  Write about...
  - what they look like
  - how they move
  - how they talk
  - their personalities

"My name is Oz," bellowed the burly caveman. Wiry hairs sprouted from his ears and yellow teeth crowded his mouth. His clothes were tattered and frayed, and he waddled as he walked...

Dramatic writing

To make your writing exciting...
  - keep your sentences short and punchy
  - use lots of different verbs
  - avoid using too many adverbs

The hungry chameleon had spotted its prey. It inched along the leaf. It aimed its mouth. With a flash of pink, its tongue shot out...

Conversation

- Try not to use the word 'said' every time you write what someone says.
- Look for alternatives on page 32.
- Think about the way your character is talking, to help you to choose the right word.

"Why did you do that?" snapped Lily.

"I'm sorry," whimpered Ant.

"I've never been so happy." bragged Henry.

Word games

These games are for two or more people to play.

A-Z game

- Choose a category such as food.
- Everyone then has to say a type of food that begins with each letter of the alphabet, starting with 'A'.
- You could make the game trickier by deciding that everyone must describe their word with an adjective beginning with the same letter.

Other categories:

Animals
Hobbies
Names
Places

Story chain

- Take turns saying one word at a time to make up a story.
- See how far you can go until someone can't think of a word.

Tip: words such as 'but' and 'however' will help you to continue the story.

Word duel

- Pick a word from the list on the right.
- You have two minutes to think of, and maybe write down, as many words with a similar meaning as you can.
- Then take turns saying one word at a time until someone runs out of ideas.

Words:

hot
cold
happy
sad
good
bad
tasty
beautiful
big
small
eat
scary
nice
run
said

hot

balmy

sweltering

sultry

humid

stuffy

warm

?

? ?

Word association

- Whoever goes first says a word.
- The next person has to say another word linked to that word.
- Each player has to keep saying a word associated with the word before it.

For example:

boat...   beach...   sand...   castle...   knight...   horse...

Word finder

If you want to find alternatives to a particular word, you can look it up in this word finder. It will tell you where there are other words to use instead.

a

ability *(noun)*
see **power**, 98
see **skill**, 74

about *(adverb)*, 37

abroad *(adverb)*, 58

accelerate *(verb)*
see **speed**, 56

accident *(noun)*, 57
see **luck**, 90

ache *(noun)*
see **pain**, 61

act *(verb)*
see **behave**, 60
see **perform**, 29

activity *(noun)*
see **hobby**, 72

add *(verb)*
see **pour**, 71

admire *(verb)*, 100

admitted *(verb)*
see **confessed**, 32

adult *(noun)*, 18

adventure *(noun)*, 84
see **mission**, 100

aeroplane *(noun)*
see **plane**, 53

afraid *(adjective)*, 35
see **scared**, 17

age *(noun)*, 88

aggressive *(adjective)*
see **fierce**, 86

aim *(verb)*
see **shoot**, 95

air *(noun)*, 53

aircraft *(noun)*
see **plane**, 53

airy *(adjective)*
see **chilly**, 65

alarm *(noun)*, 27

alarmed *(adjective)*
see **scared**, 17

alert *(adjective)*, 100

alien *(noun)*, 95

almost *(adverb)*
see **nearly**, 37

always *(adverb)*, 36

amaze *(verb)*, 98

amazed *(adjective)*
see **surprised**, 17

amazing *(adjective)*
see **incredible**, 98

amount *(noun)*, 71

amuse *(verb)*, 76

ancient *(adjective)*
see **old**, 52, 92

anger *(noun)*, 84

angry *(adjective)*, 17

animal *(noun)*, 22

announced *(verb)*
see **spoke**, 32

annoy *(verb)*, 103

annoyed *(adjective)*
see **cross**, 17

answered *(verb)*, 32

anxious *(adjective)*
see **worried**, 17

applaud *(verb)*
see **cheer**, 100

area *(noun)*, 40

argue *(verb)*, 89

arrange *(verb)*
see **organize**, 71

arrest *(verb)*, 90

ashamed *(adjective)*
see **sorry**, 17

asked *(verb)*, 32

asleep *(adjective)*, 35

astonish *(verb)*, 84

astonished *(adjective)*
see **surprised**, 17

astronaut *(noun)*, 94

athlete *(noun)*, 74

atmosphere *(noun)*
see **air**, 53

attach *(verb)*
see **join**, 63

attack *(verb)*, 47, 86, 95
see **invade**, 89

attractive *(adjective)*, 18

avenue *(noun)*
see **road**, 56

awake *(adjective)*, 35

awful *(adjective)*, 83

awkward *(adjective)*
see **clumsy**, 16

b

babies *(noun)*, 38

baby *(noun)*, 18

babyish *(adjective)*
see **childish**, 16

back *(noun)*, 37

bad *(adjective)*, 15

bad-tempered *(adjective)*
see **grumpy**, 16

bag *(noun)*, 66
see **luggage**, 58

baggy *(adjective)*
see **loose**, 67

band *(noun)*
see **group**, 78

bang *(noun)*, 27, 95

bang *(verb)*
see **knock**, 28, 60

bare *(adjective)*, 67

bark *(verb)*, 24

bashful *(adjective)*
see **shy**, 16

battle *(noun)*, 101

beach *(noun)*, 44

bear *(verb)*, 39
see **carry**, 28

beast *(noun)*
see **animal**, 22
see **monster**, 102

beat *(verb)*, 75
see **stir**, 71

beautiful *(adjective)*
see **attractive**, 18
see **nice**, 13

become *(verb)*, 25
see **get**, 30

bed *(noun)*, 34

begged *(verb)*
see **asked**, 32

behave *(verb)*, 60

believe *(verb)*, 12

bend *(verb)*, 28

best *(adjective)*, 74

better *(adjective)*, 12

beware of *(verb)*, 84

big *(adjective)*, 5

bike *(noun)*, 59

bit *(noun)*
see **piece**, 63

bite *(verb)*
see **eat**, 68

bitter *(adjective)*, 70
see **cold**, 33

blaze *(verb)*
see **burn**, 87

blend *(verb)*
see **mix**, 80

blob *(noun)*, 71

block *(noun)*, 63

bloom *(verb)*
see **open**, 38

boast *(verb)*, 99

boat *(noun)*, 54

body *(noun)*, 19

bog *(noun)*, 41

bold *(adjective)*
see **brave**, 100
see **bright**, 7

book *(noun)*, 72

border *(noun)*
see **edge**, 8

bored *(adjective)*, 17

boring *(adjective)*, 16

boss *(noun)*, 73

bounce *(verb)*
see **jump**, 28

box *(noun)*, 71

boy *(noun)*
see **child**, 18

brainy *(adjective)*
see **clever**, 16

A B C D E F G H I J K L M N O P Q R S T U V W X Y Z

brave *(adjective)*, 16, 100

bravery *(noun)*
see **courage**, 100

bread *(noun)*, 69

break *(verb)*, 28

breezy *(adjective)*
see **windy**, 33

brick *(noun)*
see **block**, 63

brilliant *(adjective)*
see **good**, 14

bright *(adjective)*, 7, 49
see **clever**, 16
see **sunny**, 33

bring *(verb)*
see **carry**, 28

brittle *(adjective)*
see **delicate**, 10

broken *(adjective)*, 57

brush *(verb)*
see **clean**, 65

brutal *(adjective)*, 102

bug *(noun)*
see **illness**, 60
see **insect**, 25

build *(verb)*, 38, 63

building *(noun)*, 62

bulky *(adjective)*
see **big**, 5
see **heavy**, 10

bump *(noun)*
see **lump**, 60

bump *(verb)*
see **knock**, 28, 60

bump into *(verb)*
see **crash into**, 57

bumpy *(adjective)*, 10

burn *(verb)*, 87

burst *(verb)*, 27
see **flash**, 95

bushy *(adjective)*
see **thick**, 46

busy *(adjective)*, 44

button *(noun)*
see **switch**, 81

buy *(verb)*, 40

C

calm *(adjective)*, 41

cancel *(verb)*, 58

capture *(verb)*
see **arrest**, 90
see **catch**, 50

car *(noun)*, 56

care *(verb)*
see **mind**, 12

care for *(verb)*
see **keep**, 43
see **look after**, 60

caring *(adjective)*
see **kind**, 16

carry *(verb)*, 28

case *(noun)*
see **luggage**, 58

castle *(noun)*, 101

cat *(noun)*, 24

catch *(verb)*, 50, 60
see **arrest**, 90

cave *(noun)*, 87

centre *(noun)*
see **middle**, 8

certain *(adjective)*
see **sure**, 80

chair *(noun)*, 64

champion *(noun)*
see **winner**, 74

chance *(noun)*
see **luck**, 90

character *(noun)*, 16

charge at *(verb)*
see **attack**, 86

charm *(verb)*, 84

charming *(adjective)*
see **lovely**, 16

chase *(verb)*, 47
see **follow**, 28

cheat *(verb)*, 75

check *(verb)*
see **inspect**, 73

cheeky *(adjective)*
see **naughty**, 16

cheer *(verb)*, 100

cheerful *(adjective)*
see **happy**, 17

chequered *(adjective)*, 9

chest *(noun)*, 96

chew *(verb)*
 see **eat**, 68

child *(noun)*, 18

childish *(adjective)*, 16

chilly *(adjective)*, 65
 see **cold**, 17, 33

choose *(verb)*, 92

chop *(verb)*
 see **cut**, 63

choppy *(adjective)*
 see **wavy**, 96

chubby *(adjective)*
 see **fat**, 5

city *(noun)*
 see **town**, 40

clammy *(adjective)*
 see **humid**, 33

clap *(verb)*
 see **cheer**, 100

clean *(adjective)*, 41
 see **tidy**, 65

clean *(verb)*, 65

clear *(adjective)*, 10, 78
 see **clean**, 41
 see **sunny**, 33

clever *(adjective)*, 16

climb *(verb)*, 28, 46, 98
 see **rise**, 53

clock *(noun)*, 36

close *(verb)*, 65

cloth *(noun)*
 see **fabric**, 67

clothes *(noun)*, 66

cloudy *(adjective)*, 10, 33

club *(noun)*, 72

clumsy *(adjective)*, 16

clutch *(verb)*
 see **grip**, 28

clutter *(noun)*
 see **mess**, 65

coarse *(adjective)*
 see **rough**, 11

coat *(noun)*, 66
 see **layer**, 63

coil *(verb)*
 see **wind**, 46

cold *(adjective)*, 17, 33, 39

collect *(verb)*
 see **pick**, 87
 see **pick up**, 29

collision *(noun)*
 see **accident**, 57

colour *(noun)*, 7

colourful *(adjective)*, 7

combine *(verb)*
 see **mix**, 80

comfort *(verb)*
 see **soothe**, 61

comfortable *(adjective)*
 see **cosy**, 65

common *(adjective)*
 see **general**, 12

competitor *(noun)*
 see **athlete**, 74

complicated *(adjective)*, 9
 see **difficult**, 71

computer *(noun)*, 72

confessed *(verb)*, 32

confident *(adjective)*
 see **sure**, 80

confirm *(verb)*
 see **prove**, 80

confused *(adjective)*, 17

connect *(verb)*
 see **join**, 63

considerate *(adjective)*
 see **kind**, 16
 see **polite**, 16

construct *(verb)*
 see **build**, 63

contestant *(noun)*
 see **athlete**, 74

control *(verb)*, 53

control *(noun)*
 see **switch**, 81

cook *(verb)*, 71

cool *(verb)*, 71

cool *(adjective)*
 see **cold**, 17, 33

correct *(adjective)*
 see **right**, 12

costume *(noun)*
 see **clothes**, 66

A
B
C
D
E
F
G
H
I
J
K
L
M
N
O
P
Q
R
S
T
U
V
W
X
Y
Z

delicate (adjective), 10

delicious (adjective)
see **tasty**, 70

delighted (adjective)
see **happy**, 17

delightful (adjective)
see **lovely**, 16

demonstrate (verb)
see **prove**, 80

den (noun)
see **nest**, 52

depart (verb)
see **leave**, 29

depressed (adjective)
see **sad**, 17

design (noun)
see **pattern**, 67

design (verb)
see **invent**, 80

dessert (noun), 68

destroy (verb)
see **break**, 28

develop (verb)
see **grow**, 38

diagram (noun)
see **plan**, 63

diary (noun), 72

die (verb), 28

different (adjective), 60

difficult (adjective), 71

difficulty (noun)
see **problem**, 61

dig (verb), 63

dim (adjective), 82
see **stupid**, 16

dip (verb), 44

dirt (noun)
see **mud**, 52

dirty (adjective), 67

disappear (verb)
see **fade**, 78
see **vanish**, 84

disaster (noun), 99

discover (verb), 88
see **find**, 28

disease (noun)
see **illness**, 60

disgusting (adjective), 70

distant (adjective)
see **faraway**, 37

disturbed (adjective)
see **scared**, 17

dive (verb), 28, 75

diver (noun), 50

divide (verb), 8
see **cut**, 63

dizzy (adjective), 17, 60

do (verb), 31

doctor (noun), 60

dog (noun), 24

doze (verb)
see **sleep**, 35

drab (adjective)
see **dull**, 7

draw (verb), 72

dreadful (adjective)
see **awful**, 83

dream (noun), 34

dreary (adjective)
see **boring**, 16

dress (noun), 66

dribble (verb)
see **drip**, 80

drift (verb)
see **glide**, 53

drink (noun), 68

drink (verb), 68

drip (verb), 80

drive (verb), 56

drop (verb)
see **sink**, 50

dry (adjective), 10, 49

dull (adjective), 7
see **boring**, 16
see **cloudy**, 33

dusty (adjective)
see **dry**, 49
see **messy**, 65

e

eager (adjective)
see **excited**, 17

earth (noun)
see **mud**, 52

easy (adjective), 71

A
B
C
D
E
F
G
H
I
J
K
L
M
N
O
P
Q
R
S
T
U
V
W
X
Y
Z

eat (verb), 68

edge (noun), 8

eerie (adjective)
see **spooky**, 82

effect (noun), 80

elect (verb)
see **choose**, 92

emotion (noun)
see **feeling**, 17

end (noun)
see **back**, 37

enemy (noun), 100

energetic (adjective)
see **lively**, 16
see **sporty**, 74

enjoy (verb)
see **like**, 12

enormous (adjective),
see **big**, 5
see **huge**, 86

entertain (verb)
see **amuse**, 76

enthusiastic (adjective)
see **excited**, 17

equipment (noun), 75

escape (verb), 90

even (adjective), 9, 43
see **smooth**, 11

evening (noun), 36

evil (adjective), 83, 95
see **bad**, 15

exactly (adverb), 37

excited (adjective), 17

excuse (verb)
see **forgive**, 93

exercise (noun)
see **sport**, 74

exhausted (adjective)
see **tired**, 17, 35

exhibition (noun), 72

expedition (noun)
see **mission**, 100

explode (verb), 87
see **burst**, 27

explore (verb), 94

extra (adjective), 71

extraordinary
(adjective)
see **incredible**, 98

f

fabric (noun), 67

face (noun), 18, 76

fade (verb), 78

faint (adjective)
see **dizzy**, 17, 60
see **dull**, 7
see **mild**, 70

fair (adjective), 12

fairly (adverb)
see **quite**, 5

fall (verb), 28, 39
see **decrease**, 39

false (adjective)
see **wrong**, 12

famous (adjective), 78

fantastic (adjective)
see **incredible**, 98

far (adverb), 37

faraway (adjective), 37

farm (noun), 42

fashion (noun), 67

fashionable (adjective),
67

fast (adjective), 56

fasten (verb)
see **join**, 63
see **tie**, 67

fat (adjective), 5

fed up (adjective)
see **bored**, 17

feel (verb)
see **touch**, 29

feeling (noun), 17

fetch (verb)
see **pick up**, 29

few (adjective), 5

field (noun), 43

fierce (adjective), 86
see **brutal**, 102

fight (noun), 90

fight (verb), 93, 100

figure (noun)
see **body**, 19

fill (verb), 71

film (noun), 72

g

A
B
C
D
E
F
G
H
I
J
K
L
M
N
O
P
Q
R
S
T
U
V
W
X
Y
Z

A B C D E F G H I J K L M N O P Q R S T U V W X Y Z

generous *(adjective)*, 16

gentle *(adjective)*
see **friendly**, 95
see **tame**, 24

get *(verb)*, 30
see **catch**, 60
see **take**, 29

get off *(verb)*, 28

get on *(verb)*, 28

get to *(verb)*
see **reach**, 29

get up *(verb)*
see **stand**, 29
see **wake up**, 35

ghost *(noun)*, 83

girl *(noun)*
see **child**, 18

give *(verb)*, 28

give up *(verb)*
see **stop**, 87

glad *(adjective)*
see **happy**, 17

glare *(verb)*
see **scowl**, 18

gleam *(verb)*
see **shine**, 94

gleaming *(adjective)*
see **shiny**, 96

glimmer *(verb)*
see **shine**, 94

gloomy *(adjective)*
see **dark**, 46
see **dim**, 82
see **sad**, 17

glossy *(adjective)*
see **smooth**, 11

glow *(verb)*
see **burn**, 87
see **shine**, 94

glum *(adjective)*
see **sad**, 17

go *(verb)*, 30
see **leave**, 29

go down *(verb)*
see **sink**, 50

go round *(verb)*, 94
see **turn**, 81

go under *(verb)*
see **sink**, 96

go up *(verb)*
see **rise**, 53

god *(noun)*, 92

good *(adjective)*, 14

good-looking
(adjective)
see **attractive**, 18

grab *(verb)*
see **steal**, 90
see **take**, 29

grand *(adjective)*, 84

greasy *(adjective)*, 70

great *(adjective)*
see **good**, 14

grin *(verb)*
see **smile**, 18

grip *(verb)*, 28
see **hold**, 84

groan *(verb)*
see **creak**, 82

group *(noun)*, 78
see **crowd**, 89
see **gang**, 90

grow *(verb)*, 38

grubby *(adjective)*
see **dirty**, 67

gruesome *(adjective)*
see **awful**, 83

grumpy *(adjective)*, 16

guard *(verb)*, 100

guide *(verb)*
see **lead**, 29

guilty *(adjective)*
see **sorry**, 17

h

hair *(noun)*, 19

hairy *(adjective)*
see **furry**, 23

handsome *(adjective)*
see **attractive**, 18

hang *(verb)*, 39

hang down *(verb)*
see **dangle**, 46

happen *(verb)*, 80

happy *(adjective)*, 17

hard *(adjective)*, 10,
39, 52
see **difficult**, 71

harm *(verb)*
see **hurt**, 60

harmful *(adjective)*
see **poisonous**, 80

hat *(noun)*, 66

hate *(verb)*, 12

have *(verb)*
see **keep**, 43

have to *(verb)*, 31

haze *(noun)*
see **mist**, 39

health *(noun)*, 60

healthy *(adjective)*
see **well**, 61

heap *(noun)*
see **pile**, 63

heat *(verb)*, 71

heavy *(adjective)*, 10

height *(noun)*
see **size**, 63

help *(verb)*, 99

helpful *(adjective)*
see **nice**, 13

hide *(verb)*, 47
see **cover**, 39

high *(adjective)*, 27, 48

hill *(noun)*, 41

hit *(verb)*, 75
see **knock**, 60
see **punch**, 99

hobby *(noun)*, 72

hold *(verb)*, 84
see **carry**, 28

hole *(noun)*, 41
see **crack**, 63

home *(noun)*
see **house**, 64

honest *(adjective)*, 16

hopeful *(adjective)*
see **sure**, 80

horrible *(adjective)*
see **bad**, 15

hot *(adjective)*, 17, 33, 49, 70
see **spicy**, 70

house *(noun)*, 64
see **building**, 62

hover *(verb)*
see **fly**, 47
see **glide**, 53

howl *(verb)*
see **scream**, 83

hug *(verb)*, 28

huge *(adjective)*, 86
see **big**, 5

humid *(adjective)*, 33
see **wet**, 46

hungry *(adjective)*, 17

hunt *(verb)*
see **chase**, 47
see **search**, 46

hurt *(verb)*, 60

hurt *(adjective)*
see **upset**, 17

hut *(noun)*, 41

i

icy *(adjective)*
see **cold**, 39

identical *(adjective)*, 8

ill *(adjective)*, 17, 60
see **sick**, 61

illness *(noun)*, 60

imaginary *(adjective)*, 84

immature *(adjective)*
see **childish**, 16

immediately *(adverb)*, 36

important *(adjective)*, 12, 88

increase *(verb)*, 38

incredible *(adjective)*, 98

injure *(verb)*
see **hurt**, 60

inquisitive *(adjective)*
see **curious**, 16

insect *(noun)*, 25

inspect *(verb)*, 73

instructions *(noun)*, 71

intelligent *(adjective)*
see **clever**, 16

intend *(verb)*
see **plan**, 92

interested *(adjective)*
see **curious**, 16

A
B
C
D
E
F
G
H
I
J
K
L
M
N
O
P
Q
R
S
T
U
V
W
X
Y
Z

A
B
C
D
E
F
G
H
I
J
K
L
M
N
O
P
Q
R
S
T
U
V
W
X
Y
Z

A B C D E F G H I J K L M N O P Q R S T U V W X Y Z

muddy *(adjective)*
see **dirty**, 67

muggy *(adjective)*
see **humid**, 33

mumbled *(verb)*
see **whispered**, 32

murder *(verb)*
see **kill**, 28

muscular *(adjective)*
see **strong**, 98

musician *(noun)*, 78

muttered *(verb)*
see **whispered**, 32

mysterious *(adjective)*
see **strange**, 82

n

naked *(adjective)*
see **bare**, 67

narrow *(adjective)*
see **thin**, 5

nasty *(adjective)*
see **evil**, 95
see **unpleasant**, 102

naughty *(adjective)*, 16

near *(preposition)*, 37

nearly *(adverb)*, 37

neat *(adjective)*, 67
see **tidy**, 65

need *(verb)*, 31

nest *(noun)*, 52

next *(adverb)*, 36

nice *(adjective)*, 13

night *(noun)*, 34

nightmare *(noun)*
see **dream**, 34

nimble *(adjective)*, 98

noise *(noun)*, 27

noisy *(adjective)*, 27

nosy *(adjective)*, 16

notice *(noun)*, 41

now *(adverb)*
see **immediately**, 36

nude *(adjective)*
see **bare**, 67

o

obedient *(adjective)*
see **tame**, 24

ocean *(noun)*
see **sea**, 96

odd *(adjective)*
see **strange**, 82

offer *(verb)*
see **give**, 28

often *(adverb)*, 36

okay *(adjective)*, 15

old *(adjective)*, 18,
52, 82, 92

ooze *(verb)*
see **drip**, 80

open *(verb)*, 38
see **undo**, 67

opinion *(noun)*, 12

opposite *(preposition)*,
37

ordered *(verb)*
see **shouted**, 32

ordinary *(adjective)*, 12

organize *(verb)*, 71

p

pain *(noun)*, 61

painful *(adjective)*
see **sore**, 61

paint *(verb)*
see **decorate**, 65

pale *(adjective)*, 61
see **dull**, 7

part *(noun)*
see **piece**, 63

party *(noun)*, 72

passage *(noun)*
see **tunnel**, 88

path *(noun)*, 41

pattern *(noun)*, 67

pay *(verb)*
see **spend**, 40

peaceful *(adjective)*
see **calm**, 41

peculiar *(adjective)*
see **strange**, 82

peer *(verb)*
see **look**, 29

perform (verb), 29, 78

perhaps (adverb)
see **maybe**, 12

personality (noun)
see **character**, 16

pester (verb)
see **annoy**, 103

petrified (adjective)
see **afraid**, 35

photo (noun), 72

pick (verb), 87
see **choose**, 92

pick up (verb), 29

picture (noun), 72
see **photo**, 72

piece (noun), 63

pile (noun), 63

place (noun), 37
see **area**, 40

place (verb)
see **put**, 29

plain (adjective), 9
see **ugly**, 18

plan (noun), 63

plan (verb), 92
see **organize**, 71
see **prepare**, 58

plane (noun), 53

plant (noun), 20

plastic (noun), 10

play (verb), 38, 75
see **perform**, 78

pleasant (adjective)
see **nice**, 13

pleased (adjective)
see **happy**, 17

pleasure (noun)
see **fun**, 72

poisonous (adjective), 80

poke (verb), 29

polish (verb)
see **clean**, 65

polite (adjective), 16

poor (adjective)
see **bad**, 15

port (noun), 44

possible (adjective), 12

post (noun), 41

poster (noun)
see **notice**, 41

pounce on (verb)
see **attack**, 47

pour (verb), 71

power (noun), 98

powerful (adjective), 93
see **fast**, 56
see **strong**, 86

practical (adjective)
see **sensible**, 16

practise (verb), 78

prepare (verb), 58
see **practise**, 78

press (verb)
see **push**, 29

pretty (adjective)
see **attractive**, 18

prickly (adjective)
see **spiky**, 49

problem (noun), 61

prod (verb)
see **poke**, 29

promise (verb)
see **swear**, 100

proper (adjective)
see **fair**, 12

protect (verb)
see **defend**, 99
see **guard**, 100

proud (adjective), 16, 99

prove (verb), 80

pull (verb), 29
see **close**, 65

punch (verb), 99

pure (adjective)
see **clean**, 41

pursue (verb)
see **chase**, 47
see **follow**, 28

push (verb), 29

put (verb), 29

put on (verb)
see **wear**, 67

puzzled (adjective)
see **confused**, 17

A
B
C
D
E
F
G
H
I
J
K
L
M
N
O
P
Q
R
S
T
U
V
W
X
Y
Z

q

quarrel *(verb)*
see **argue**, 89

quest *(noun)*
see **mission**, 100

queue *(noun)*, 40

quick *(adjective)*
see **fast**, 56

quickly *(adverb)*, 32

quiet *(adjective)*, 27, 34
see **calm**, 41

quietly *(adverb)*, 32

quit *(verb)*
see **stop**, 87

quite *(adverb)*, 5, 37

r

race *(verb)*
see **rush**, 47

rainforest *(noun)*
see **jungle**, 46

rainy *(adjective)*, 33

raise *(verb)*
see **lift**, 75

rather *(adverb)*
see **quite**, 5

rattle *(verb)*
see **shake**, 29

ravenous *(adjective)*
see **hungry**, 17

raw *(adjective)*, 70

reach *(verb)*, 29

ready *(adjective)*, 58

real *(adjective)*, 84

really *(adverb)*
see **very**, 5

rebel *(verb)*, 93

receive *(verb)*
see **take**, 29

recover *(verb)*, 61

regular *(adjective)*
see **even**, 9

relax *(verb)*, 72
see **rest**, 35

religion *(noun)*, 92

remove *(verb)*
see **take off**, 67

repair *(verb)*
see **fix**, 10

rescue *(verb)*
see **save**, 99

rest *(verb)*, 35

restaurant *(noun)*, 40

result *(noun)*
see **effect**, 80

retreat *(verb)*, 100

revolting *(adjective)*
see **awful**, 83
see **disgusting**, 70

rich *(adjective)*, 88
see **bright**, 7

right *(adjective)*, 12

rigid *(adjective)*
see **hard**, 10

ring *(verb)*, 27

rise *(verb)*, 53
see **stand**, 29

risky *(adjective)*
see **dangerous**, 48

river *(noun)*, 41

road *(noun)*, 56

roar *(verb)*, 27
see **crash**, 96

robber *(noun)*, 90

rotten *(adjective)*
see **bad**, 15

rough *(adjective)*, 11
see **tough**, 102
see **wavy**, 96

row *(noun)*, 43

rub *(verb)*
see **smear**, 103

rubbish *(noun)*
see **litter**, 41

rude *(adjective)*
see **bad**, 15

ruin *(verb)*
see **break**, 28

run *(verb)*, 29

runny *(adjective)*, 80

rush *(verb)*, 47

ruthless *(adjective)*
see **cruel**, 100

S

sad *(adjective)*, 17

said *(verb)*, 32

sail *(verb)*, 96

salty *(adjective)*, 50

sample *(verb)*
see **taste**, 70

satisfied *(adjective)*
see **full**, 17

savage *(adjective)*
see **brutal**, 102
see **fierce**, 86

save *(verb)*, 99

scamper *(verb)*
see **run**, 29

scare *(verb)*, 83
see **shock**, 103

scared *(adjective)*, 17

scary *(adjective)*
see **spooky**, 82

scowl *(verb)*, 18

scramble *(verb)*
see **climb**, 46

scrape *(verb)*
see **scratch**, 86

scratch *(verb)*, 86

scratchy *(adjective)*
see **sharp**, 11

scream *(verb)*, 83

scrub *(verb)*
see **clean**, 65

scruffy *(adjective)*, 67

sea *(noun)*, 96

seabed *(noun)*, 50

search *(verb)*, 46
see **explore**, 94

seat *(noun)*
see **chair**, 64

section *(noun)*
see **piece**, 63

seem *(verb)*, 12

see-through *(adjective)*
see **clear**, 10

seize *(verb)*
see **steal**, 90
see **take**, 29

sensible *(adjective)*, 16

separate *(verb)*
see **divide**, 8

serious *(adjective)*,
16, 61

serve *(verb)*, 71

shabby *(adjective)*
see **scruffy**, 67

shadowy *(adjective)*
see **dark**, 34, 46
see **dim**, 82

shady *(adjective)*
see **dark**, 46

shaggy *(adjective)*
see **fluffy**, 10

shake *(verb)*, 29, 81,
83
see **wave**, 29

shape *(verb)*
see **make**, 63

sharp *(adjective)*, 11, 96
see **bitter**, 70

shatter *(verb)*
see **break**, 28

shed *(noun)*
see **hut**, 41

shelter *(noun)*, 87

shine *(verb)*, 94

shiny *(adjective)*, 96

ship *(noun)*
see **boat**, 54

shock *(noun)*, 90

shock *(verb)*, 103
see **surprise**, 90

shoes *(noun)*, 66

shoot *(verb)*, 95

shop *(noun)*, 40

short *(adjective)*, 5

shouted *(verb)*, 32

shove *(verb)*
see **push**, 29

show *(verb)*
see **prove**, 80

shriek *(verb)*
see **scream**, 83

shrivel *(verb)*, 38

shudder *(verb)*
see **shake**, 81

shut *(verb)*, 29
see **close**, 65

A
B
C
D
E
F
G
H
I
J
K
L
M
N
O
P
Q
R
S
T
U
V
W
X
Y
Z

trick *(noun)*, 76

trickle *(verb)*
  see **drip**, 80

trip *(noun)*
  see **journey**, 58

trip *(verb)*
  see **fall**, 28

trouble *(noun)*
  see **danger**, 89
  see **problem**, 61

trousers *(noun)*, 66

truck *(noun)*
  see **lorry**, 56

true *(adjective)*
  see **real**, 84
  see **right**, 12

truthful *(adjective)*
  see **honest**, 16

try *(verb)*, 31
  see **taste**, 70

tug *(verb)*
  see **pull**, 29

tumble *(verb)*
  see **fall**, 28

tunnel *(noun)*, 88

turn *(verb)*, 81
  see **spin**, 77

turn on *(verb)*
  see **start**, 56

twist *(verb)*, 29
  see **spin**, 77
  see **wind**, 46

type *(noun)*, 53

typical *(adjective)*
  see **general**, 12

U

ugly *(adjective)*, 18

underwater *(adjective)*, 50

undo *(verb)*, 67

unemployed *(adjective)*, 73

uneven *(adjective)*
  see **rough**, 11

unfair *(adjective)*, 12

unpleasant *(adjective)*, 102

untidy *(adjective)*
  see **messy**, 65

unusual *(adjective)*
  see **special**, 12
  see **strange**, 82

upset *(adjective)*, 17

V

vain *(adjective)*
  see **proud**, 16

vanish *(verb)*, 84

vast *(adjective)*
  see **big**, 5

vegetable *(noun)*, 69

very *(adverb)*, 5

vicious *(adjective)*
  see **fierce**, 86

vile *(adjective)*
  see **evil**, 83

villain *(noun)*, 99

violent *(adjective)*
  see **tough**, 102

vivid *(adjective)*
  see **bright**, 7

W

wail *(verb)*
  see **scream**, 83

wake up *(verb)*, 35

walk *(verb)*
  see **go**, 30

want *(verb)*, 31

warm *(adjective)*
  see **cosy**, 65
  see **hot**, 33

wash *(verb)*
  see **clean**, 65

watch *(verb)*
  see **guard**, 100
  see **look**, 29

wave *(noun)*, 96

wave *(verb)*, 29
  see **flick**, 50

wavy *(adjective)*, 96
  see **zigzag**, 9

weak *(adjective)*, 61
  see **dizzy**, 17

A B C D E F G H I J K L M N O P Q R S T U V W X Y Z

X Y Z

Usborne Quicklinks

To visit websites where you can find more writing tips and word games to play, go to the Usborne Quicklinks website at www.usborne.com/quicklinks and type in the keywords 'junior thesaurus'.

When using the internet please follow the internet safety guidelines displayed at the Usborne Quicklinks website. The recommended websites are regularly reviewed and the links at Usborne Quicklinks are updated. However, Usborne Publishing is not responsible and does not accept liability for the content or availability of any website other than its own. We recommend that children are supervised while on the internet.